A B C Club

End of an Era

Sunny W.

ISBN: 978-1-4834-4351-5 (sc)
ISBN: 978-1-4834-4349-2 (hc)
ISBN: 978-1-4834-4350-8 (e)

Library of Congress Control Number: 2015920559

Because of the dynamic nature of the Internet, any web addresses or links contained in this book may have changed since publication and may no longer be valid. The views expressed in this work are solely those of the author and do not necessarily reflect the views of the publisher, and the publisher hereby disclaims any responsibility for them.

Any people depicted in stock imagery provided by Thinkstock are models, and such images are being used for illustrative purposes only. Certain stock imagery © Thinkstock.

Lulu Publishing Services rev. date: 4/18/2016

ACKNOWLEDGEMENTS

My heartfelt thanks to the co-founders of Alcoholics Anonymous, Bill Wilson and Dr. Bob, without whose wisdom and dedication this book would not be possible.

Many thanks to my husband, Bill, for his knowledge gained during his 23 years of service with the club. He was a big, big help. To Helen Leahy, my mentor, and sponsor who started me writing the history of the ABC Club and it ended up being a book. Candice B. who edited the history of the ABC Club and had familiarity with the club, her father being the co-founder. David B for his cover drawings. To the persons who gave me interviews of their experience at the ABC Club. Tears were shed, and laughter was abundant. Danny for being, well, Danny. My children who helped and encouraged me, and all of you who made this book possible.

For Danny and Helen Leahy
Who made life worth living

CONTENTS

CHAPTER 1

History

You're probably wondering why I would care about the ABC Club Recovery and Rehabilitation Center and its history. Well, because the ABC Club, along with Danny and Helen Leahy, saved my life and the lives of hundreds more.

After I had a seizure in a Mobil gas station restroom, the paramedics came and took me to Desert Hospital in Palm Springs. I was diagnosed as having had a LSD flashback, and I was physically, spiritually, and emotionally bankrupt. In August of 1981 I went into recovery at the ABC Club in Indio, California. Who would have known it was the best thing that ever happened to down-and-out for-the-count me?

To paraphrase an announcement at the ABC Club Friday Night Speaker Meeting is, 'If you are busted, disgusted and can't be trusted, you would be welcomed at the ABC Club.'

The ABC Club is not affiliated with Alcoholics Anonymous. The club is a place where many come for help, and some to live while getting healthy, clean, and sober. It holds a variety of Twelve Step meetings such as AA (Alcoholics Anonymous), Al-Anon (family and friends of alcoholics), Ala-teen, (teenage children of alcoholics), NA (Narcotics Anonymous), CA (Cocaine Anonymous) CODA (Co-dependents Anonymous), OA (Overeaters Anonymous), ACA (Adult Children of Alcoholics), Gamb-Anon (Gamblers Anonymous), and SA (Smokers Anonymous). The attendees of the meetings pay rent, for the space, for their meetings. A basket is passed and people at the meeting put in

1

a dollar or two. If they're broke, like a lot of newcomers are, nothing is expected. Each month a certain percentage generated from each meeting is given to the club for rent.

In the past the ABC Club also had many of its own groups; such as one called the Hot Seat were residents evaluated each other, with a facilitator present. It was not a pleasant experience, and some sought revenge when the other's turn came to be evaluated. Another group was Women Who Love Too Much. Aftercare classes were held in the evenings for the residents, and former residents.

The term used in the club name was taken from the Big Book of AA:

A. That we were alcoholic and could not manage our lives.

B. That probably no human power could have relieved us of our alcoholism.

C. That God could and would if he were sought.

These thoughts were published in 1939. The AA principles have been used in managing the club since its founding in 1962.

For the purpose of anonymity individuals in this book are referred to by first names and last initials only (unless they are deceased, not alcoholic, or not addicted).

The ABC Club became a reality in March of 1962 when Howard Bibby moved from Texas to the Coachella Valley. Located in the Southern California desert. At that time he had almost two years of sobriety. Shortly after he arrived he attended his first AA meeting in the desert at the local Episcopal church, on a Monday. Five people were there. He met a man there named Charles (Chuck) Loogs, who said they needed to get a facility to get drunks off the streets. Howard liked the idea. He'd previously seen a similar club in Texas, where he had gotten sober. Chuck and Howard planned to pattern it along those same lines.

They contacted John Peters who owned a two-story adobe house located on Miles Avenue in Indio. It had a basement and a swamp cooler, and the walls were eighteen inches thick. Once the house was cooled, even in July and August, it stayed cool. In summer the California desert heat can reach more than 120 degrees. John lent the adobe to Howard and Chuck for the new house for drunks.

Howard and Chuck started the ABC Club with a bunch of donated chairs and beds. The sleeping quarters were upstairs. The living room on the main floor was used as the meeting room. Two removable tables were put up in the living room for breakfast, lunch, and dinner, and after each meal they were taken down. The charge for room and board was $13 a week. If the men wanted to have a room, and no food, because some of them worked in local restaurants, cafes, or hotels, and could eat where they worked, the charge was only $8 a week. The rent included laundry facilities provided via two beat-up old washing machines in the back yard.

At that time, there was a group of homeless bums between Indio and Coachella. About thirty to one hundred of them camped along the railroad tracks, depending on what time of the year it was. The Coachella Valley is mostly a seasonal destination. Occasionally the ABC Club would have one, or two homeless who were tired of their way of life. Some of the residents living at the club worked as caddies. The Southern California desert was beginning to become a golfer's paradise.

About two months after opening, due to neighbor's complaints, the Indio District Attorney came to see Howard. The DA wanted to know why he shouldn't arrest him and Chuck for contributing to the delinquency and degradation of the community, by allowing "those kind" of people to come in from Skid Row. Howard took a sergeant from the Indio Police Department, and a member of the DA's office for a tour, after that they realized the ABC Club wasn't as bad as the neighbors had said.

The first year things went along well. The average occupancy was from one to five men. Meetings were held on Tuesday and Friday nights. In addition Howard and Chuck would take residents of the club to Palm Desert for a Saturday Night Speaker's Meeting at the Palm Desert Community church. The meetings at the Episcopal church, where Howard and Chuck met, had closed because two of the men got drunk. Persons pursuing sobriety relapsing was not uncommon, as they would learn in the future.

In 1963 the club had it's first seven-member board of director's meeting. By fall of the second year residency increased from seven, or eight residents to ten. No one would have guessed, that in the coming

3

years the club would house from up to 178 residents. In the summer of 1963, Chuck told Howard they would never be any bigger then they were. He added that he wanted to close the facility down because he was going to be gone, for an extended vacation.

Howard and Chuck did not live there. They shared the care of the residents: Howard would go by at lunch and make sure the residents had something to eat (they ate a lot of bologna sandwiches) and in the evening Chuck would check on them.

Howard told Chuck that he would be there all summer and that he wanted to try to keep it open. They had two people all summer, and kept it open. Fall of the second year, there were a bunch of men-old, drunk, and homeless-who would come from the railroad tracks and sleep upstairs.

In the beginning there were only AA meetings. The house rules required that any man who stayed for two weeks had to get a job. There was a restaurant called Vance's Filling Station, which was owned by Vance Y. Vance was always good to take care of two, or three guys washing dishes. At one time he probably had eight dishwashers, from the club, when he only needed one. He was also good about giving the club leftover food. The club survived. It never occurred to them that they couldn't.

Right after Christmas of the third year a lady named Lucille arrived and the club now had its first woman member. Lucille stayed sober and was active in the club a couple of years. When she moved away, the distance made it hard to get to meetings. She no longer was as active in the club after the move.

When Connie L went to her first AA meeting at the club. She entered through the back door. She said about twenty people were there, laughing and having a good time. Whoever was leading the meeting was telling about a Mexican fellow resident who couldn't speak English, so he would sleep on his AA Big Book, hoping to get the program by osmosis.

According to Connie the club had a busted sofa that had one big spring sticking out in the corner. If someone sat down they'd be okay, but if they moved that spring would gouge them. The members would put the newest guy on that end of the sofa and tell him to sit quietly.

About the time he'd get relaxed and start dozing, that spring would bring him to attention.

Danny was executive director of the ABC Club. Connie would tell people that she was Danny's mother and many believed her. Danny played along and told people she was his mother. The residents were astonished when they learned the truth. This deception went on for a lot of years. Danny and Connie loved getting this one over on residents, and attendees of the meetings.

In May 1963 John Peters told Howard he needed the property to build a hotel, he added that he had another house for the ABC Club. One that was built in 1929 by Max Royce and his father. Originally the Peter's homestead. Howard and Chuck bought a lot on Biskra Street and then negotiated with a mover to move the house to the new location. The cost for the move (including plumbing and set up), was $3,500.

Shortly after the move they resumed operations. At this time Connie and her husband Triff became a very important cog in the wheel. It's likely without their constant attention to the day-to-day operation, as well as their efforts to secure donations, the whole ABC Club may have failed. Connie and Triff held it together.

A few months after the move to Biskra Street the ABC Club was incorporated. A lawyer, who came to speak at the Friday Night Speaker Meeting in August of 1963, drew up the non-profit status, at no charge.

Al McCandless was on the Riverside County Board of Supervisors. He helped the ABC Club get a grant of $37,000 (which was a huge amount of money then): one could have bought a very nice house for half that. Al supported the ABC Club as long as he was on the board of supervisors.

The little one story front house, a duplex, eventually become the ABC Club Bunkhouse. Two families lived there and paid $250 a month rent. That helped meet expenses. There were seven or eight residents living at the ABC Club. They had outside jobs and those that could pay, did. The bunkhouse, in later years, became a study and resident staff rooms.

In 1968 a nucleus of about five, or six persons supported the ABC Club. They were lucky in that whenever they needed things done they would always have a drunk in the ABC Club, getting sober, that could do whatever needed to be done. They had a plumber when plumbing was needed, carpenters when carpentry was needed, and usually always had somebody in residency who could cook.

Bob McCandless later came on the Riverside Board of Supervisors. He was also a champion of the ABC Club helping in any way he could.

When there weren't meetings at the club, the people that supported it would get together at each others homes, and bake cakes, and have a great time sober. Howard said those were crazy times. Once they had a drunk whose wife had dropped him off. They put him on one of the upstairs bunk beds, and proceeded to have a meeting. As the meeting was going on for about an hour, he fell out of bed three, or four times. They would run upstairs and hoist him back up. Finally they realized with their alcoholic wisdom, if they'd put him on the bottom bunk, he wouldn't be so hard to handle. The next day, they asked him how he felt? He said, "I never knew I'd have such a hangover from getting sober."

There was a group of people that donated to the ABC Club. Howard said a lot of people were involved. Betty Munday and Dottie Chicon. Polly Wentworth got involved when Jim Metcalf asked her to do an assessment so Riverside County could give county funds to the ABC Club. The ABC Club had a good reputation because they were helping homeless drunks. Homeless drunks were a different breed of alcoholics. For one thing, they weren't always very clean and nobody wanted them around. That's why the ABC Club was started.

Chuck was operating the ABC Club at that time. His brother and brother's wife then operated it for awhile. Chuck's brother was the first volunteer manager that lived in the club. Howard Bibby resigned from the ABC Board. Years later, Howard would be on the ABC Board again, and serve for 25 years.

The ABC Club was soon mortgaged to the hilt. The club was in bankruptcy, and in the process of foreclosure. When it went up for auction, the group whose members supported ABC got a loan from a savings and loan association, and bought it back.

In 1969 the first Valentine's Day dinner dance was held, and a television was raffled to raise funds. This started the fund raising trend of many dinners, dances and raffles to follow.

CHAPTER 2

Danny's Arrival

In 1969 Danny Leahy arrived by bus in Indio. He made a phone call from the Greyhound Bus Station. He intended to call AA but instead reached the ABC Club. The men there invited him over the next morning. He showed up in the morning and had coffee with some of them. His next stop was at the Indio Parole Department because they had a job waiting for him.

Danny lived in Coachella and attended meetings, on Tuesday, Friday and Sunday night at ABC. Fred managed the ABC Club. When Danny had been around about a year, Fred invited him to move into the club. Danny had been hanging around some slippery spots in Cathedral City and he didn't want to drink, so he accepted the invitation and moved in.

Fred had a habit of retiring to his room at 7:30 on non-meeting nights. One night Danny came home late, about 11:00, and four guys were sitting on the couches drinking wine. Danny raised hell, and threw them all out. Fred was not pleased about that, but Danny didn't care. After that the joke around the ABC Club was, 'Don't worry about the manager, but watch out for Danny.' This occurred in 1970 and set a precedence for many years.

Danny stuttered when he talked. The kind of stuttering that made people want to finish his sentences for him. People thought that this was most likely why he kept conversations short, sweet, and to the point.

During his early days at the club Danny worked driving a catering truck for Vance's Catering. Vance in turn donated a lot of food to the ABC Club. Other community citizens, and John Peters donated hams and turkeys every Thanksgiving and Christmas. Now a fellowship member, Connie was always out running a raffle of some kind, or another. A lot of people were involved with helping the ABC Club. Donations kept the ABC Club afloat for years.

When Danny had been at the club about a year and a half, he met Helen who had been going to meetings there. Helen was a beautiful blond who wore short skirts. She resembled Doris Day. Danny and Helen started going to outside meetings together. One of the meetings was called 'Young Action for Under Forty.' Thirty was considered young in those days. After six months dating Danny got up the nerve to ask Helen to marry him. She said, "No," that she did not want to get married again. He thanked her, went back to the ABC Club and told Fred he was going to San Francisco, because the terms of his parole were that he had to stay in the desert six months, and he had fulfilled his commitment.

Helen called Danny the next day, and told him she had changed her mind, and she would marry him. They were married February 1971 at the club.

The ABC Club Board asked Danny to be temporary manager, but they could only pay him $1 a day. There was no more money available, but it was important to everyone involved to keep the ABC Club going.

In July of 1971 Helen was voted to be on the ABC Club Board of Directors. Helen also worked as a caterer for Vance's Catering. She learned a lot about the catering business, and in the following years she organized many holiday meals at the ABC Club, and at Fellowship Hall in Palm Desert. She also played a big part in organizing the Madd Dog Daze Convention. It was held at the desert Date Festival Fair Grounds in August in Indio. Mostly locals attended.

Helen and Connie ran and cleaned the ABC Club. Sometimes they moved the furniture and pictures so often that the guys would come in, and just flop on the floor, tired of trying to figure out how the place was going to be arranged. One time the ladies found a liquor bottle under some towels, in a dresser in the corner bathroom while they were cleaning. They never did find who it belonged to. Nobody would confess.

Connie and Helen had bake sales, and sold pens with praying hands. Usually outside of the Gemco Store on Monroe Street. They did anything to make a buck in order to feed the guys. If it hadn't been for all the food Vance Young donated, they may have starved. Vance was a real caring person; anything for the ABC Club.

There were a lot of residents, three to each room, and three, or four on the couches. The beds and couches were always full. And then there was the floor; the men would get a blanket and plop on the floor. The ABC Club Board was always worried that they would get in trouble for having too many residents. Danny never turned anyone down.

Senator Harold Hughes appropriated money for recovery homes. Margaret Denton was real interested in the ABC Club. Dale Winn was the first coordinator for the Riverside County Alcohol Control Program. In those days the Riverside County Alcohol Program and Riverside County Drug Program were completely separate. However, today they are bound. There is just one office now. Margaret Denton got books from the California Association of Alcohol Recovery Homes. Dale put all the money into what's called the Desert Alcohol Coalition in Palm Springs. It was a convalescent hospital to begin with. Through the efforts of Margaret and others the only way you could get any funding from Riverside County was to be licensed and certified. That is what Helen and Margaret worked on, and the ABC Club got licensed and certified. Then the ABC Club was certified by the state also.

In 1973 it was decided that Danny would be the one to decide how long a person could stay.

And the Food Stamps began to go directly to Danny.

In 1975, the ABC Club received enough money from the county to put an addition on. Plans were made and carried out to add on to the front of the house, to have a larger meeting, and eating area. The addition is visible because you can easily see there is a big beam across the living room ceiling. Helen had the furniture and podium moved on a regular basis. One never knew how it would look when they showed up for the next meeting. Helen enjoyed rearranging everything. She was quite the arranger.

In 1978 the ABC Club got a grant to bring the house up to code. They upgraded the program. There were fourteen men. Helen finally was able to get a telephone in her office. It was an extension of the phone she had at home. Coffee prices went up. Danny, to save money, would get Postum, or Amaretto Coffee from Mexico. There were a lot of complaints. It was awful. Danny would say, "And I hope you don't like it." The daily turkey baloney sandwiches for lunch were tolerable.

Also in 1978 Riverside County approached them about treating women. Women were able to reside in the main house. Soon after there were three women upstairs. The manager at that time was real strict and watched out to make sure that nothing improper took place. Fraternizing was against the rules of the ABC Club which made it a constant challenge. Love often bloomed at the club. Danny would say, "Two sickies don't make a wellie."

The club hired a bookkeeper. In February the rent was raised to $42 room and board, $27 for board $15 for food.

Danny and Helen resigned from the board as their board membership conflicted with their role as employees. Howard Bibby came back as president of the ABC Board. The Riverside County and California State staff came to discuss the program. They wanted to start more houses patterned after the ABC Club.

About 1979 the Recovery Home Guidelines stated that recovery homes needed to have a resident council. Three of the residents decided that they would start a ABC Club Resident Council. The staff wasn't allowed in the resident council meetings unless they were invited to be there. Part of the social model is all about the residents participating in their recovery, and running the house as much as possible. The resident council developed the recreational activities. They held dances. They participated in the suggestions of running the ABC Club. They had fund raisers to get money for cigarettes, sundries, trips to Magic Mountain, and to the Alcoholic Olympics. There were picnics and baseball games. The residents recycled cans for cash. Every weekend they would have a car wash. It was very popular, perhaps because the girls were scantily clothed, and soaking wet, than it was to solely support the ABC Club residents.

In those years everybody that smoked, smoked indoors. Sometimes our eyes would burn and leak from all the smoke. One day Danny decided to quit smoking, and he forbade it in the ABC Club buildings.

The smokers thought that was a bummer, and the non-smokers were delighted. Danny was so ornery when he quit that Helen told him if he didn't shape up she would get a divorce. He shaped up somewhat.

At night after the meetings Danny would gather together residents to go for mandatory, healthy long walks around the neighborhood. What a sight that was, all of them walking along like some gang taking over. Often the mascot dogs of ABC would join in on the walk.

People associated with the ABC Club, their friends, and neighbors donated clothes, furniture, and dishes to ABC. The residents called the donations, 'donos.' They would go through the donos and take what they needed, or wanted. There were verbal fights over some of the donos. Seniority prevailed, when two or more persons wanted the same thing. Residents would also hoard stuff to take with them when they moved. A senior resident was placed in charge of the donos, to sort things out. There was a monthly yard sale that the residents operated. The money collected from the yard sales went to fund the resident council.

In the mid 1980's girls had a two foot closet each, so clothes were stashed under the twin bed mattresses. That also kept them nicely pressed. Each female resident had a three drawer dresser. For shoes the girls removed the bottom dresser drawer, put the shoes on the floor, and put the drawer back.

The club had a dress code that was stringently enforced. For the girls no short shorts; longer shorts and Bermuda shorts were acceptable. The girls were required to wear a bra. One of my experiences was, when the nosy, tattletale girls told Helen that I was not wearing a bra, Helen said, "Oh, that's alright for Sunny." I weighed one hundred eight pounds when I arrived at the club, and had nothing going for a bust line.

The men had to wear a shirt at all times. We did however, unbeknown to Danny, have a life size poster from the hips up of Tom Selleck without a shirt, only Levis. It hung on the wall over one bed in the small girl's house. He was our eye candy.

The ABC Club Resident Council paid for cigarettes for the residents. The cigarettes were kept in a locked metal cabinet. Whoever was in charge for the week would divvy out the packs one at a time. The local Indians at that time had a tobacco store in Indio so residents had runs to get the cigarettes. They were less expensive from the Indians.

11

When I moved out of the ABC Club, after nine months residency, my first apartment was furnished with mostly donos. My wardrobe was also made up of donos. As the years went on, when I could donate whatever, it made me feel good to see residents wearing, and using my discards, and the rest going to be sold. The yard sales featuring donos were one of the more lucrative fund raisers for the residents.

The resident council also paid for the feeding and care of the dogs. There were always one, or two dogs that showed up at the ABC Club, and stayed. In 1985, Helen and Danny had a black standard poodle, named Frenchy. He would walk to work with them everyday. They lived about a block from the ABC Club on Tahquitz Street. Frenchy liked to jump from bed-to-bed in the girls seven bed bedroom. Drove us nuts. Frenchy disappeared one day. Helen felt that someone stole him. Then there was Peanuts who was a little, fat, light brown Chihuahua mascot. And later there was Wino, my favorite, who was a small black terrier mix. The last dog I knew of was Fred, a huge St. Bernard who became a regular. Helen would often scold the residents for feeding the dogs at the table during meal time. The dogs would get too fat. The dogs knew they were special because of the residents loving on them constantly. In return they provided unconditional love, companionship, entertainment, and a listening ear.

There were four regular AA meetings at the ABC Club at that time. Residents were transported to outside meetings, held at Fellowship Hall, every weekday morning, and to the Saturday Night Speaker Meetings. The ABC Club held groups every weekday. Polly Wentworth, who was an alcohol/drug counselor with Riverside County Alcohol Control, held a Women's Luncheon Group every Tuesday. Polly made the women aware of relapse triggers, and helped the girls to build their self esteem. When Polly retired Sharon Koski, Family and Marriage Counselor, became the facilitator. One time at the luncheon, Susan Van Winkle slipped out of her chair, and had a major withdrawal seizure, making a good case for sobriety. The paramedics came and hauled her off to JFK Hospital in Indio. She was the house mother at the ABC Club Doll House for quite a while, and also worked for Howard Bibby at the Awareness Drinking Driver Program with me. She later died of esophageal cancer.

Marian Rickert Family and Marriage Counselor later was hired to counsel residents one on one, and facilitate the Tuesday Luncheon Group. Helen always attended the luncheon. Sharon Koski Family and Marriage Counselor had moved to Wisconsin.

Danny held weekly, 'Pack Your Shit Meetings.' The meetings were mandatory. It always started with, "I didn't come in here to win friends and influence people; I came because alcohol was killing me and I need to remember that." The roll was checked, and Danny asked each resident if they wanted to be there. Any problems were brought to light. He reminded them, "No fraternizing. No she-ing and he-ing, or she-ing and she-ing, or he-ing and he-ing. If one's getting some then everyone should be getting some, because if their not somebody is going to tell." Danny told them why they were there and what's expected. "It's not a motel, or hotel, it's a recovery home. You asked me to let you come in. I didn't ask you." Then he inquired if there is anything the staff, or himself, can do for them. Rules were established. Any person leaving the ABC Club with a member of the opposite sex would under no circumstances be readmitted. They would be referred to another facility. There was not so much paperwork then and there was a concentration on dealing with the residents; more hands on and camaraderie.

Danny had a lot of one liners that were classic: "Bring the body, and the mind will follow." "Don't act guilty if your not guilty." For the girls, "He is not Prince Charming" and "He is not Mr. Wonderful." "We are alcoholics helping other alcoholics put their lives back together." "Act as if." "Lack of sleep never killed anybody." "Alcohol was kicking my ass." "You don't have to live in a recovery home to stay sober (when he kicked someone out of ABC)." "ABC is not the bedrock of mental health." "God runs the club, we just show up." "There are no bars on the windows, or doors, you are free to leave any time." "You can't get anybody drunk, and you can't get anyone sober. You're not that powerful." "Carry the message, not the alcoholic." "Stinking thinking will get you drinking." "It's none of your business what anyone thinks of you."

Another classic Danny had, paraphrased from the Twelve Steps and Twelve Traditions AA book, "I would rather believe in God and get up there and find there isn't one, then to not believe in God and get up there and find out there is one."

If the residents were at the ABC Club for 'three hots and a cot,' they didn't last long, Danny was very perceptive and quickly weeded out the non-compliers.

For the regular Twelve Step Meetings, Danny was a stickler about us sitting still in the meetings. He would say, "Go to the bathroom, and get yyyour coffee, or soda. I dddddon't want to see anyone get up during the meeting." Although, Danny was lenient with the pregnant girls when they needed to use the restroom.

Cars were occasionally donated to the club and Danny would give the cars to the residents that he felt had been deserving. No money ever changed hands.

Each week at the Pack Your Shit Meeting someone would be awarded the Pity Pot. It was a large brown, ugly, ceramic toilet with Pity Pot written on it. The residents would nominate candidates and the group would vote on it. Sometimes alcoholic/addicts feel very sorry for themselves. They like to wallow in self pity. Poor me, poor me, pour me a drink. Self pity often was a relapse trigger. After I had moved out of the ABC Club, Danny sent word for me to attend the PYSM and I thought something special was going on. It was to grace me with the Pity Pot. Thanks a lot Danny. Polaroid pictures were taken and posted on the walls. Later on a collage was made out of the photos and hung on the wall to remind us of how good we had it since the picture had been taken.

One of the rules that existed in the club was one that appeared to be out of line in relationship to other rules, that were simple to understand and accept. The rule I'm referring to is called horse play. What Danny and Bill found out, over the course of time, was that horse play inevitably led to a physical altercation between the two horse play participants. As the result a rule was established that if you were engaged in horse play, both participants would be asked to leave. While this may seem harsh to some people it enforced the policy of the ABC Club that it was a safe place to recover in.

New residents were restricted to the property for thirty days, so they could concentrate on their recovery without any outside influences. That meant no phone calls made, or taken, no visits by family members, nor significant others. They could write, or receive mail that the staff did not open, or censor. If someone screwed up, such as low riding (bullying) another resident, Danny would increase the restriction time to sixty days, sometimes ninety days. Some residents were restricted to the grounds, for one year. It was a choice, jail, prison, or the ABC Club, as dictated by the court.

After a resident's restriction was up they were allowed to have their kids at the ABC Club for the weekends. A good number of residents had lost custody of their children. The court, or family services would allow weekend visits, and the residents were very grateful to continue, or rebuild relationships with their children. The ABC Club also held parenting classes for parents in the club, and outsiders that were in a mandatory, either or else situation. Some residents lost custody of their children permanently.

ABC Outreach program was every Wednesday, Thursday and twice on Friday. George H started the program. When he got married and left, Ken Earhart took over. They would take a group of residents to assemblies and health classes in the local high schools. They targeted the kids who were starting to have problems with drugs. The residents and Ken would share their stories, of despair and recovery, in the hope that it would give the students at risk something to think about. Some of the students would write gratitude letters to ABC about what they had gotten out of the group's sharing. He was proud of the letters.

While I was a resident, in 1983, George H was the Outreach coordinator and I was fortunate to be able to go with the panels. Although, when we went to Indio High School, where my son was a student, he requested that I not let anyone know I was his mother.

By now they had regular recreation activities for the residents that included horse shoes, baseball, potlucks, and bowling. Harvest Bowl in Indio furnished shoes and charged $20 weekly for the whole group. Dances were held on special holidays like Halloween, and residents would wear costumes. Also St. Patrick's Day, Christmas etc. Alcoholics were learning to be social, instead of being loners.

For three, or four years, ABC had a bread run every morning where the residents would take Danny's truck and pick up day old left over bread, tortillas, and pastries at Von's and Ralph's. The club would take what they needed to feed the residents and the rest would go to the neighbors. The stores eventually, after about three years, stopped the practice.

Jim Metcalf was the coordinator for Riverside Alcohol Control. Plans had been made by Polly Wentworth and Jim Metcalf, to go co-ed. Due to Helen the club got an IRS/ID for non-profit status. She was very inexperienced at such forms. She filled it out as best she could and sent it in. They called her on the phone and corrected this, and that, until it was right. Helen then went to Chapman University and got her CADAC (California Association of Drug and Alcohol Counselors).

In 1979 Bill W drove up in his dirty brown Pinto, fell out, and staggered into the club. There sat Danny, who stuttered, and Bud Chaney with his foot up in a cast. Bill wondered what he had got himself into. In 1981 Bill became the ABC Club's CFO, and was later an ABC Board member.

Bill W sold his Pinto to one of the residents, who sold it to me. Bill told me to make copies, and give him all the papers, and he would take care of registering the car. Then Bill decided to experiment some more, and he took a sabbatical. By then the Pinto was only firing on three cylinders. When I went to register it I didn't have a pink slip, or the title to the car. I knew nothing about car titles. After making some phone calls I learned a bank in South Carolina held the title. Howard Bibby advised me to offer the bank fifty dollars for the title and they accepted.

Bill W returned to the desert in 1987. He pursued serious sobriety and again became CFO of the ABC Club. He and I were married in 1991. While living at the club I worked cleaning houses with Kay Stinson, also a resident. Bill asked her if she would ask me if I would go out with him. I told her to ask him if his finger was broken (before cell phones). He finally called me, and we started dating.

There were probably bets being placed about our marriage and if it would last, or not. Bill W is a business man, and I'm a tomboy. We had known each other for quite a few years. My sponsor was not real happy about our union. She thought we should have gone together longer. We have been married twenty-four years and counting.

Danny and Helen had a Gremlin at that time and always made it available to transport men and women to the assorted appointments they had, for example doctors, dentists, parole officers, probation officers, and jobs. It was also used for us to drive to our housecleaning jobs. Later on they had an old yellow station wagon that we used for our cleaning work.

The cooks would fix us brown bag lunches to take to work, as long as we signed up the night before. Usually we had peanut butter and jelly, or turkey baloney sandwiches, and goodies from the bread run. On the weekends the cooks would make a large breakfast for the residents. During the week it was cold cereal. One of the girls must have thought we were a high end outfit because she wanted to know where the croutons were for her dinner salad. Tuesday was Mexican food night. Friday usually was fish sticks night. The cooks were big on a weekly meatloaf night too.

I really appreciated not having to cook while I was at the ABC Club. It freed my mind up to be able to concentrate on sobriety.

There were many occasions when both male and female residents were offered the opportunity to work outside the club. However, one of the problems they ran into was that the residents in many instances were paid very low wages. The reason for this was the thinking in those people's minds that because residents were living in a recovery home they would not need much money. Danny finally laid down the law that when people went out to work, they were to be paid.

CHAPTER 3

Running the Club

Andy Anderson, a benefactor, loaned the club $20,000 and the board purchased the house across the alley and the ABC Club went co-ed. An ABC friend was instrumental in getting the women who owned it to sell. In the early 1980's times were tough for the women residents. The small women's house had seven beds in one long bedroom, a small kitchen, and a tiny bedroom for the house mother. The girls shared one bathroom. One of the wickeder house mothers would get upset because the girls had to go through her bedroom to get to the bathroom. She accused us of intentionally bumping into her bed as we passed by in the middle of the night. She made life miserable. I was on scrub the kitchen floor duty, on hands and knees, for two solid weeks. It was not cool to whine to Helen, because if we did things would just get worse. The housemother's name was Pat and we later became friends. Sadly, she had a stroke and later died.

We also were not allowed to flush the toilet while a girl was showering, because the hot water would scald whoever was in the shower.

Neatness was mandatory. Helen would personally inspect the girl's house daily and dispose of our things that were laying around. She would put them in a box and if you were lucky you would get them back. Each girl had a chore: to scrub the bathroom, to mop the floor, vacuum, dust, clean the fridge out, or rake the yard. The chores would change each week. The resident council elected a sergeant of arms to make sure chores were completed. He would walk around with his clipboard, making notes and supervising. The men also had their chore lists to complete and be checked.

Once a month would be deep cleaning. Walls, windows, and anything that needed scrubbing got the works. Helen also made sure we girls made our beds each morning. And anyone late for the morning meetings would suffer the wrath of Danny. We girls would have a meditation circle in the morning, at our little house, before the day got started. Years later a large bathroom, with two more showers, were added to the girl's house and it became the detox center.

It should be noted that the men became more concerned about their appearance, and cleaned up their language, somewhat, after the women's house filled up. I had been a beautician in my previous drinking/drugging life and I was elected to cut the resident's hair, and I also cut Danny and Helen's hair for a few years. Danny would pay me $3 for each of the resident's haircuts. I told him I would do it for free, but he insisted. The haircuts helped the resident's self esteem; and it helped my coffee and cigarette habit. One time I cut seven, or eight stitches from a man's scalp. It appeared the stitches had been there for a long while. They were embedded in his head and had to be pulled out. The man had come from a hobo camp at the railroad tracks. He was grateful to have the stitches removed, and get a decent haircut

The ABC Club was usually, seemingly always, overcrowded, with some of the newer alcoholics sleeping on the living room couches, and on the floor. The ABC Club Board was always holding their breath hoping that Danny wouldn't get caught for having over his limit of people. There was a great family closeness because they were all in one building. Everybody knew everybody and there was nowhere to hide. They either got the program, or were sent down the road.

There was a gay fellow in the house and he would come prancing down the stairs in his pink fuzzy slippers and pink bathrobe with his hair up in curlers. Imagine him among the ex-cons and hard core alcoholic/addicts. But he was happy to be who he was. He had a big crush on Danny. There was a conglomeration of people in the club. They were only concerned with alcohol and drug recovery; they were not concerned with sexual orientation, race, color or creed. Helen, who manned the office, referred to the residents as a big dysfunctional family.

A lot went on during those times in front of everyone: Residents had DT's (delirium tremors) in the living room. Often someone would be lying on the couch puking their guts out into a bucket, or shaking like a giant vibrator, with withdrawal. Having them in the living room helped remind the residents where they came from. That was Danny's idea.

We only had one death at the ABC Club that I know of. His name was George and he was an older man who had tried to commit suicide by shooting himself in the stomach with a shotgun, but he didn't die. He came to the ABC Club, got sober and died of pneumonia.

The women's Thursday Night Candlelight Meeting that was originally held in the small women's house quickly outgrew it. Then it was moved to Danny and Helen's house, outgrew it, and moved over to the main women's house. It rapidly outgrew the women's house, and moved to the Leahy Building, where it is to this day.

My experience with recovery is: I stopped using drugs and drinking alcohol on August 7, 1981. I had a spiritual experience, which consisted of my showing up for an AlAnon Meeting that wasn't scheduled that night due to the Maad Dog Daze Convention being at the County Fair Grounds. The alcoholics invited me to join them in their meeting. I believe God opened a window in my soul and let me know that I was the alcoholic. I was the problem.

I went cold turkey, and had a seizure, diagnosed as a LSD flashback, and ended up in Palm Springs Desert Hospital for seven days. I had pulled out the marijuana plants I was growing so I wouldn't be tempted, much to the consternation of my fair-weather friends. Arlyn Rudolf and another lady picked me up, at the end of the week, and drove me straight to the ABC Club from the hospital. They did not stop at my house for clothes and make up. I only had the clothes that I went to the hospital with.

The first thing Helen did, when I got to the ABC Club, was to have me lay and listen to meditation cassette tapes, to calm me down. One of the senior girls went to Gemco and bought me underwear. A couple of days later, my then husband Boyd brought, a suitcase with some of my clothes and makeup in it.

Danny would tell new residents that ABC was the last house on the block, or the bottom of the barrel. I told Danny it was a step up for me, and it was. My first stay was only five weeks because I had a thirteen-year-old son at home, and Boyd that I was married to at that time, was into alcohol and drugs heavily, as I had been. Because he could drink more than me, and do more drugs, I had been in deep denial.

Danny told me that he knew where I was coming from. It took me a while to process that I was coming from way behind. Alcoholic/addicts like me, in our disease are immature, full of self pity and despair. We stunted our emotional development when we begin drinking and using. For me it was when I was fourteen. I was a high school drunk. In my high school yearbook there are a few references to my drinking from friends that signed it. Two wrote 'To the drunken sophomore.' One reference was to my drinking, smoking, and swearing too much and the short life I was going to have. I was clueless. In retrospect it makes sense.

At the ABC Club, when the men and women's houses were full, waiting lists were started. The Sunday night meeting became a candlelight meeting. All attempts to purchase the lot next to the ABC Club on Biskra were futile. But in 1982 two tiny houses on Palm Street were purchased, and plans materialized to build a large facility. Funds were received from the Bob Hope Chrysler Classic, the Gannett Foundation, the McCallum Desert Foundation, and private donations.

The first architect had one floor. In the beginning it was just going to be a new kitchen, offices, a dining hall, and meeting room. In 1986 the ABC Club Board decided in mid-stream it would be foolish not to add more beds upstairs. The first architect resigned and the board hired a new architect to do the upstairs. Luckily the first architect had built the foundation good so that it could accommodate a second story. Another Bill W, who was a painting contractor, stepped up to the plate, and hired sub-contractors to finish the building.

The ABC Club rented a duplex that was in turn rented to residents ready to leave the ABC Club, but still felt they wanted to be in a safe and stable environment. It was known as the Three-Quarter-House. The duplex was at the end of the alley on the corner of Valencia Street and Palm about a hundred feet from the ABC Club. Three or four guys lived in each side. The Three-Quarter-House soon became self supporting,

21

and had a maximum stay of six months. Later ABC acquired three sober living homes through HUD, a couple of miles away from the club. The ABC Club is located in a rough neighborhood.

In 1983 the ABC Club Alumni Association was formed and the monthly alumni speaker meeting breakfasts started to be held on the first Sunday of each month. Breakfast was served and the profit of the funds raised were for the current residents. The money was used for trips to 6 Flags Magic Mountain, and funding for the yearly retreats. Retreats were held in Idyllwild, a mountain community, Pinion Pines, half way up the mountain, and San Felipe, Mexico. The retreats were facilitated by alcohol and drug counselors. Those in attendance had wonderful times getting to know each other better, and learning to deal with living as a clean and sober person. Many laughs were had during contests to see who had moved the most during their disease, or who had been married the most. The residents learned to accept their past and know that they cannot go back.

It was important for residents to learn to socialize, to get along with each other, with all the different personal idiosyncrasies. Getting along with people in the club meant getting along better in the outside world.

The ABC Alumni held a outdoor barbecue fund raiser every April. There were pie eating contests, one legged races and other events. The dunk tank always made a lot of money. Many of the residents and alumnus' got a thrill out of trying to dunk Danny. The staff took their turn too at being dunked. They all thought that was huge fun. After the festivities and meals, there was an AA Speaker Meeting.

CHAPTER 4

Party Time

Christmas at the ABC Club was a huge event. Danny would dress up as Santa Claus. With his beard grown longer, and his Santa suit, he looked like the real Santa. The attendees at the Christmas party would sit on his lap, and get their picture taken with a Polaroid camera. Danny played Santa Claus at the Christmas party for many years. Some times a live band played the music and other times the party planners hired a disk jockey.

The music was always loud. Lots of finger food was available for everyone.

The female alumnus' would give the girls a private Christmas party before the Thursday night Women's Candlelight Meeting. It was a lot of fun shopping for the girls, and reminiscing about experiences at the ABC Club. Most of the money for the presents came from people that supported the club. Connie would always give a generous check. Hallmark would send Helen little keepsakes for the girls that we included in their gift bags. Warm socks, fingernail polish, make-up, shampoo, conditioner, earrings, brushes and combs were welcomed presents.

We made the girl's Christmas party a potluck, with a lot of the female alumnus' bringing side dishes, turkey and ham, and too many desserts. The current chef at ABC would cook the turkey and ham for us.

The ABC Club would chip in and give the alumni money for the men's presents, and we girls would do the wrapping. The men's gifts were usually a different color sweatshirt every year, with the ABC logo, and the year, in the upper left hand corner, a plaid flannel long sleeve shirt, and shaving gear. The Always Believe in Children program was started to give the children of residents an annual Christmas party. There were gifts from (Danny) Santa Claus, and goodies for all the resident's and alumnus' children. There were also Easter egg hunts at Easter and baskets of candy and toys for each child. In the summer, the children received scholarships for a week at camp. Usually the YMCA camps.

CHAPTER 5

My Story

When I had two years of sobriety I divorced my then third husband, Boyd Lemmon. I had thought if I was clean, sober, warm, and wonderful, he would get clean and sober and we would ride off into the recovery sunrise together. He had no intention of quitting drugs, alcohol, and womanizing. Because I was broke, Inland Legal Services helped me with the divorce paperwork. It was my second divorce from him. The papers were served when he was in the Indio Jail.

That husband, Boyd, had a violent cold sore on his lower lip that turned out to be melanoma cancer. He suffered horribly with extensive surgeries for three years. He got an infection and the doctors wouldn't do any more surgery. We did a geographic, moving from Utah to California.

Eight years after I divorced Boyd I met the women he married after me. She had divorced him, and was now in recovery. We became friends, with a friendship that lasts to this day. We both knew the hell the other had experienced. Not only was Boyd a full blown alcoholic/addict but he was very verbally abusive. I told myself that I drank and used to keep my sanity. It backfired on me. Boyd's former wife said that the only good thing that came from her marriage to him was our friendship. Boyd died on Oct. 3, 1995.

I had moved around many times in my youth. I was born moving and I was a suitcase child. I was born in Manitowoc, Wisconsin and lived in Oshkosh, Fond de Lac and other Wisconsin cities, as well as cities in Minnesota, South Dakota, Nevada and Utah. Finally I moved to Southern California, living in La Quinta, Palm Desert, and finally Indio.

In Salt Lake City I moved approximately thirteen times to different suburbs. My three children went to different schools almost every year. As a youth I lived with various relatives and in foster care. So therefore, I stopped getting attached to people and places. It was easy, in a way, to get divorced and move on. It was natural to befriend people and leave them. Until recovery I did not stop moving, and didn't have roots, or permanent relationships. I've now been in Indio over thirty years, and have a permanent home, a permanent husband, and permanent friends. My three children are in my life. It is a great feeling to go somewhere, such as the grocery store, or a restaurant, and see and talk to people that I know.

I've been married six times to four men. My first marriage ended because I was a party girl. I had married a sweet, nice Mormon boy. I've had a lot of remorse over that marriage and how it ended. But I have two wonderful children as a result of that marriage.

My second husband I married twice. He was already married when I married him. A fact that I didn't know, until his other wife located him and called to ask for a divorce.

My third husband, Boyd, drank and used drugs heavily. I couldn't deal with his drinking. I started going to AlAnon. I divorced him. Six months later I remarried him. That is when he developed cancer. He would come home from his hospital trips and drink, and I would take his drugs. Then in the chaos I became a daily drinker and drug user.

When I got sober I was unable to survive outside of the ABC Club because I was mentally unstable, anxiety ridden, and unable to keep a job to support myself and my thirteen-year-old son. The other two children were older and had already started their families. I had alcohol/drug psychosis. Defined by Webster's Dictionary as a severe mental disorder characterized by symptoms, such as delusions, or hallucinations that indicate impaired contact with reality. That certainly described me. I also had impending doom.

During this period while at the ABC Club my son, Brandon, came to live at the club. We had nowhere else to go. Danny made meetings mandatory for him, as they were for all the residents

After a few weeks sleeping in the car Brandon decided to come inside and sleep on the floor with the recovering drunks. That was quite an experience for him. It finally came his turn to have a bed. Danny said he was proud of him for speaking up and saying that he was next in line. The residents would steal Brandon's milk from the fridge. He would write POISON on a brown paper bag and put the milk in the bag. The residents would take it anyway. Brandon also lived in Danny and Helen's house with another one of the resident's sons for a while. During the summer he escaped the heat by staying with a friend who was a forest ranger in Rapid City, South Dakota.

In the station wagon (dubbed Kermit) I bought with money from the Riverside County Welfare Department, I transported residents to the Fellowship Hall Saturday Night Speaker Meeting, and back to the ABC Club. The car needed steering fluid daily, but it safely got us there and back.

CHAPTER 6

Expansion

In 1984 the Bob Hope Classic gave the ABC Club $10,000. Actor Ralph Waite became a valued board member, and started raising funds by putting on plays here in the Coachella Valley. He was the key force to raise money for the new men's facility. He was extremely important in getting funds. Ralph eventually became president of the ABC Club Board of Directors. Betty Ford and The Ladies of the Eldorado Country Club also contributed a great deal of funding. The ABC Club was completely paid for.

In 1985 a program called Friends of the ABC Club began. They helped in raising funds. Financing was a constant challenge. This meant that a person who is economically disadvantaged could have a bed and come in as a resident of the ABC Club.

1987, the new Men's House was completed. It was located at 44-434 Palm Street. The living quarters for the men was upstairs. The shared meeting and dining areas were downstairs with a large kitchen at one end. Danny's office adjoined the main office, and on the other end of the building was another office. The back room had been designed for Al-Anon, and they used it for a long period of time. The ABC Club had to hire more staff, and when they did that, it was necessary to turn the back room into offices. The Al-Anon people relocated in the women's house.

Tim A came to the club in 1992 and stayed on as a staff member to become the educational coordinator. When residents had thirty days they were tested to establish their educational level. For example, those residents that did not have a high school education. would be set up with classes which would enable them to obtain a GED. Tim was well aware of the importance of education and he felt that while recovery from alcoholism and drug addiction was of utmost importance, so too was education. Unfortunately many of the residents were deficient in their educational skills and this of course contributed to their inability to deal with the norms of society.

After the men were moved to the newly built house, the old house became the Women's Transition House. A house mother was hired for the transition house, and one for the women's new house, dubbed the Doll House, because it was beautifully decorated. The house mothers provided oversight to the girls and also worked in the office. The eight bed women's house became the ABC Detox Center. Newcomers were kept there five to seven days with constant surveillance to observe their health and welfare. They may, or may not go into residency in the ABC Club. It was the residents who monitored the newcomers by keeping a chart and listing their behavior. Each resident had a time slot to do their detox watch which was supervised by the detox manager. The detox watch helped remind the residents where they came from.

Bill W had a living skills class that was of an educational nature. He taught basic fundamentals of writing resumes, job interviewing techniques, how to write checks and balance a checkbook, how to deal with legal problems, telephone manners, social skills, and how to get an ID and a driver's license. Some alcoholics, especially those that had been living on the street lacked in some basic social skills. Bill felt teaching these skills would be of great importance when the residents moved on. The whole idea was to instill that while the residents were recovering from substance addictions, living skills were part and parcel of the recovery process.

Helen was program director. She established groups. She supervised control of month end reports to go to Riverside County, incoming donations and acknowledgments being sent to the appropriate persons.

In 1995 the club leased two HUD Indio homes for a year at $1 each. One home was for sober men, and one for sober women. They were on Colgate and Dartmouth Streets. Later two more were added.

In Indio, on Hopi Street was the home for men, and on Sirocco Street was a sober living home for women with children. The houses were only for residents who had gone through recovery at the ABC Club. Tim A was the coordinator.

CHAPTER 7

The Sober Life

After I moved out of the ABC Club I hung around a lot, because I wanted to stay clean and sober. I attended many meetings, and groups, sometimes as many as five each day. For the morning meeting we were transported to Fellowship Hall in Palm Desert. Back at the ABC Club at ten o'clock we had a group studying the AA Big Book, or the AA book Twelve Steps and Twelve Traditions. A Luncheon Meeting was held on Tuesdays at noon, for women only, led by a licensed Family and Marriage Counselor named Sharon Koski. There was also a three o'clock group based on the AA Living Sober book. Alcoholic/addicts can get sober, but the challenge is staying sober. The Living Sober book states that we are like pickles. We were cucumbers, and we turned into pickles. We can not go back to being cucumbers ever again, no matter how hard we might wish it. I volunteer facilitated a Living Sober group for about three years, alternately with a Twelve and Twelve group.

The club hosted a number of meetings: Monday was a free evening, Tuesday was a mixed meeting. Wednesday was the Beginner's Meeting (chips were given for thirty, sixty and ninety days, and one year). Thursday was the Men's Only Stag Meeting, and the Women's Only Meeting held in separate rooms. Fridays there was a Speaker Meeting at the club, and Saturday evening we were transported to Fellowship Hall to a Speaker Meeting. Sundays once a month was a breakfast fund raiser and Speaker Meeting.

SUNNY W.

Danny kept an eagle eye on the residents to make sure they were minding their own business and not trying to fraternize.

Elizabeth Taylor donated a van to the ABC Club and I wrote the thank you letter. Whenever I wanted to get out of going to a group, or a meeting (usually the Hot Seat) I would ask Helen if she had any typing for me to do. And she usually did. We also put out a quarterly newsletter. Before we had computers, I was Helen's main typist.

If a resident drank, or used they were kicked out of ABC. Danny let the others know that sobriety was serious business. If they stayed sober for thirty days on their own, they were allowed to come back into the club. Often when residents were tested, they would swear that they weren't drunk or loaded. When the test results came back positive they swore it was a mistake. Usually they had been ratted on by another resident, or felt so guilty they would confess.

Helen and Danny would send all the residents not on restriction to the AA conferences at the local hotels. Supporters of the ABC Club would donate registration, and whole tables for the banquet speaker meetings. Some persons would fund one or two residents. Those that didn't get funded were paid for by Danny and Helen. Eagle eye Danny would be at all the events, to make sure that the residents were on their best behavior.

While I lived at the ABC Club I was fortunate to be able to go on Twelve Step calls. An AA Twelve Step call is when a person makes a phone call desperately seeking help with their addiction to alcohol and/or drugs. Two sober alcoholics would go to where that person was located. Men worked with men, and women worked with women. They would share their story of experience, strength, and hope. The hope is that the person who called can realize that he/she is not hopeless. Sober alcoholic/addicts can many times convince the desperate one to seek help.

Danny and Helen's vehicles were generally used for Twelve Step calls. Helen took the calls and decided which residents would be most suitable to help the caller.

Once Helen got a call and sent two of us off on an adventurous trip. When we women residents arrived at the home of a girl, in her early twenties, we found her and her brother fighting. The brother had a knife, and the girl had grabbed it, and sliced her finger to the bone. We eased her out to the car and took her to the ABC Club so the nurse could look at it. The nurse and myself took her to JFK Hospital for stitches. I held her hand while the doctor sewed her finger back together. We took her back home, made sure she was safe. She had assured us she would be okay. It was scary because her brother was very irate, drunk, and ranting and raving. We carefully made our way to the car. We never did share any of our program with the girl. But later on I saw and spoke to her in a few meetings.

Another Twelve Step call was in the manager's office of a local trailer park. The manager had called Helen. She said a women was in their office drunk and they couldn't get her to leave. Well, we hurried on over and there she was! She was in her eighties and totally sloppy drunk. She hurled a lot of swearing at us. I called Helen who said she knew the lady. They had already had her in residency and did not want her back. Helen said she would call around and find her a place for recovery. We fruitlessly tried to talk some sense into her. Helen called back and said no one would have her. The other recovery homes had already dealt with her. We offered to take her to the Mission. She said no way, so we left her there. When I got back to my bed I cried and cried. I did not want to turn out to be an eighty year old drunk women that nobody wanted. So it seems that she did a Twelve Step call on me.

Later on that day a taxi pulled up and the driver pushed her out and took off. I guess the manager of the trailer park paid him to drop her off at ABC. Helen relented and let her stay. She wasn't with us very long.

Jack McGovern bought a house in Indio for the ABC Club to use as a women's house. It housed sober women, pregnant women, children, and a housemother. Four babies were born in the house, or the mothers were in labor before going to the local hospital. Mary E wrote a grant to turn the house into a daycare for alumni and residents, but it was denied. In 2007 the house was still functioning as a women and children's house, but financing it was a challenge.

CHAPTER 8

The Thrift Store

In May 2000 the ABC Club opened the ABC Thrift Store, with the business name Leather Plus. An anonymous donor, who owned a leather factory, would donate leather furnishings to the store. Wealthy persons in the desert donated whole households of home furnishings, when they sold their homes, or redecorated. They received tax benefits, and the satisfaction of seeing the results of their generosity. From the May opening in 2000 Leather Plus contributed more than $40,000 to the ABC Club in January 2001. They then had a new source of support, enabling ABC to progress with expansion plans and provide services so badly needed in the area. Over the years Leather Plus gave more than $1,000,000 to ABC's Adopt a Bed Program.

Leather Plus provided on the job training. Residents that were clean and sober were hired. They learned about salesmanship, management, and other skills needed in the working retail business. The delivery persons learned how to move furniture successfully. Helen, Gay Henchey and myself would volunteer, and arrange the furniture into little groupings in the store every Thursday. Helen had an eye of how to fit in the arrangements and decorations. One large corner of the store was dedicated to Helen with a large neon sign. She put all the antiques in her corner. Antiques were her passion.

Helen knew at that time that she had stage four advanced lung cancer. It became harder and harder for her to work. She was a fighter, and she kept showing up while she was being treated, but grew weaker.

The store and the ABC Club Board disagreed on the store's profit and contribution to the ABC Club. At the same time the economy caused the sales to dwindle. Helen wrote personal checks to help keep the store afloat. The Leather Plus Board was asked to resign, which we did, and the ABC Club Board took over the retail store, but were unable to remain open.

In January 2001 the club held the open house and dedication for the forty bed, ten bungalow Transitional Living Village located across the street from ABC's main facilities. As recovery center residents complete their stay three, six, and nine months to a year-with ABC Primary Care, they could move to the bungalows. Most residents needed to be gently transitioned to be able to ease back into society and the community. They were to obtain jobs, or enroll in school, pay rent and food costs, and stay no longer then twenty-four months.

The village is self contained, with parking, full landscaping, playground area for children, and laundry facilities. There are four bedrooms in each of the ten bungalows, with a common living room and kitchen.

In February 2001 Helen and Danny Leahy were honored at the ABC's Annual Recognition Dinner. The Ambassador Leonard K. Firestone Award of Merit and fund raiser. They were presented the honor for their involvement with drug and alcohol rehabilitation, and their devotion and service to thousands of people, assisting and participating with them in their substance abuse recovery. Ralph Waite (1998), Betty Ford (1999), and James W. West M.D. (2000), were the first three honorees.

In 2001 the ABC Club received a donation of $50,000 and started the Family and After Care Program. Bill M was hired to be the coordinator. The program recognized that chemical dependency and other addictive behavior adversely affects family members of the alcoholic/addict, often severely. Bill M increased the emphasis on family support through education at ABC. He assisted family members to focus on personal recovery.

In January 2002 the dedication was held at the new $1.5 million Helen and Danny Leahy Community-Education Center on the corner of Indio Boulevard, and Palm Street. The center was to be the new cornerstone of the ABC Campus. It was to be utilized by ABC residents, staff, and transitional residents. There were counseling rooms, a nurse's office, a resident exam room, meeting rooms, kitchen and reception area.

Also 2002 was the ABC Club's 40th Anniversary. Over three hundred persons toured, and took part in the dedication. Leonard Firestone kept the ABC Club going when times were tough. By the 40th year the club had gone from four, or five beds, to a facility that housed, educated, and rehabilitated more than one hundred fifty men, women, and children in various stages of alcohol and drug recovery.

CHAPTER 9

Co-Founder

Howard Bibby, the original co-founder died in 2006 from complications of heart disease at his home in Palm Desert. He was eighty-five years old. Besides being a co-founder of the ABC Club, Howard owned and operated a department store on Fargo Street in Indio. He also founded Fellowship Hall on Portola Avenue in Palm Desert, and started a non-profit to manage the hall. Today the hall hosts many self help meetings per month. He later developed the Drinking Driver Awareness Program in Indio and Palm Springs. He co-founded the Maad Dog Daze AA Conference held in the summer in the Coachella Valley.

I worked as a secretary/receptionist for Howard for nine and a half years. He, unbeknown to me, started a retirement account for me. I didn't know about it until toward the end of working for him. From that job I had the experience to work for Riverside County as an Eligibility Technician for Cash Aid, Food Stamps, and MediCal for fourteen years. I had gone from one side of the desk to the other side. Five of those years I uncovered fraudulent cases, processed the paperwork for the monies owed, and referred cases to the fraud investigators. I loved doing that. Now I am retired and have a decent living thanks to Howard, and Riverside County.

Howard was a veteran, having served in the Air Force's 390th Bomb Group during World War II, flying thirty-five missions over Germany as a waist gunner. He was awarded the Air Medal for his service.

Howard married Marilyn Townsley in 1940 and they had two daughters, Candace who lives in Indian Wells, California and Angela who lives in Austin, Texas. Howard and Marilyn took great happiness in knowing that the ABC Recovery Center helped many people

Marilyn Bibby died in October, 2007. She was eighty-five. Howard Bibby had forty-five years of continuous sobriety when he died, and Marilyn had thirty-three years.

His daughter Candace said, "He was an old Texan with a great sense of humor and personal strength and integrity." She said he opened the recovery center after struggling with alcohol when he was a young man.

Howard and Marilyn Bibby

CHAPTER 10

Danny Speaks

Danny Leahy's, Shades of Serenity interview with Bill M 2004. Bill M interviewed people who had found a way to continue to be of service for long periods of time in spite of all the stress involved.

When I first got sober there was no color. It was doing it, or not doing it. I got sick and tired of being sick and tired. It's been thirty-five (at time of interview) years for me. I know the price is too high for me. I'm a bar drinker. I loved going into the bars. I loved climbing up on the barstool and looking in the mirror. They always had to have a big mirror in the bar. I like waving the bartender down to tell him to give me a double.

But in order to do that I would have to put my sobriety on the bar, then my wife, and my children. My children who I abandoned. I was separated from them for fourteen years. Through God and this program I got them back in my life, and now I've got grandkids. Then they would have to go on the bar also. Besides the grandkids, I've got great grandkids. I'd have to put them up there too. The price is too high. I ain't willing to do that today.

I think I'm pretty good at helping people help themselves. That's why I do it. That's why we get up in the morning, and we go to court in the morning. Sit there. We've got to go through everything we go through to help somebody, help themselves. We did it this morning. This kid was scared to go to court. He was supposed to been in court back in August. He was out getting loaded and didn't go to court. Then

September 3rd he came into the program and he stayed here up until today and we took him to court. I told the judge that he had been in the program since September 3rd.

I believe God made everyone perfect and man came along and screwed it up. I believe circumstances put us into this position. I was told, when I was a child, that when God was passing out brains I was hiding behind the door. I think there's a lot of us hiding behind the door. We are entitled to have brains. We're entitled to do the right thing. I think a lot of us are ready for the change.

CHAPTER 11

Retirement

Things had been rolling along smoothly. All was well. Then everything fell apart. Helen's illness caused her to retire to start treatment in 2007.

In February 2008, the ABC Club Board hired a new executive director to replace Danny. As happens after a new management with a new approach comes in, Danny was let go. Bill resigned a few weeks later.

Helen, Danny and Bill did not get a pension, a dinner, a watch, or a hand shake from the board. Nothing.

The alumni had a dinner for them at Fantasy Springs Casino. The ABC Alumni presented each of them a trophy for their many years of service.

Helen died on 1/9/11 from lung cancer. The memorial was held at Leather Plus. The upstairs balcony, and the lower floor was packed with people who loved her. Helen had made a difference in their lives. She had touched them with love and kindness and sobriety.

Danny died on 2/10/13. I suspect mostly from a broken heart. He had lost his Helen, and his ABC Club. They were the two loves of his life.

His memorial packed Southwest Community Church. A huge church. So many people loved Danny.

This book has the testimony of some of the people Danny and Helen helped along the way. Others did not wish to participate. Still others have moved away and some have passed away. All of the statements that have been made by the participants in this endeavor are true to the best of my knowledge. Several of the participants in this literary piece are still active in the substance abuse community in the desert. They are among the first to concur that those who were residents of the ABC Club credit the club with helping save lives, including sometimes their own. The great strengths of the ABC Club was it's ability to allow the residents to find their own recovery.

There are also people who were not residents of the club, but were well aware of the excellent work that the club performed regardless of one's station in life. Participants have been more than willing to share their experiences while connected to the ABC Club and Danny and Helen.

Included are some of the letters that help to tell the story, and photos of the wonderful magical time we had at ABC. God truly blessed us addict/alcoholics.

This tale was written as a labor of love and appreciation for the ABC Club and Danny and Helen.

Helen & Danny

Main House

Original Women's House & me

Bunkhouse

12/99

ABC CLUB
2000

12-2001

12-2001

ABC CLUB
2002

2003

2004

2003

2005

Me with the Pity Pot

Bill with the Pity Pot

The Fire Department had a training session burning down the motel.

Then the transitional Living Village was built on the land.

Leather Plus

2001   Firestone Award Honorees

Wedding Anniversary

Special occasions

Danny's last outside meeting, and his pal Joe

Helen Leahy

Helen Leahy 71 of Indio, California, died January 9, 2011, at the home of her grandson in Grants Pass, Oregon after a long battle with cancer.

Her husband Daniel survives her as well as her 6 children, 12 grandchildren and 14 great grandchildren.

Helen recently moved to Grants Pass to be by her daughters due to her battle with cancer. She spent her life in the desert area of California. She dedicated the last 40 years to the recovery field, where she codirected an alcoholic recovery home, ABC Recovery Center, with her husband.

Helen is best known to her family for her sense of humor, and dedication to the recovering alcoholic. Her life of service did not go unnoticed, she received the Woman of the Year from Soroptomist of the Desert. Helen co-received the Firestone Award with her husband. Everyone's life became better for having known her. She not only touched lives but had ability to help change them for the better. She will be greatly missed. The world will be a less whole without her in it.

Daniel Raymond "Danny" Leahy

Daniel Leahy was born August 28, 1936, in San Francisco, Calif. He married Patricia Perry on August 31, 1957, and became father to Kathy in 1959 and Danny Jr. in 1961. He came to Southern California, and found sobriety in 1968. At the ABC Club's humble beginnings, he lived in the Biskra Street residence, and eventually took over running the Club. He met Helen Hogue there in 1969, and they married on February 24, 1971. The Board named him Executive Director, and Helen Co-Executive Director, through February 2008. The two became the faces of the ABC Club, as thousands of people passed through it, and changed their lives because of the Leahys and the ABC Club programs. Bill White, former Chief Financial Officer of the Club, said," Dealing with people, with alcoholics-nobody could ever be as effective as Danny." Leahy often participated in court, where judges developed a great appreciation for his offering residence at the ABC Club as a viable alternative to the penitentiary – with great success. As the ABC Club grew, so did Danny's reputation. He is survived by his daughter Kathy Leahy Ellison and her Husband Steve of Placerville, Calif., and their children Stephanie Dablin (32) and Stacy Ellison (31) and Stephanie's children Michael (3) and Katelyn (2). He is survived by his son Danny Leahy Tomasello of San Burno, Calif. and his children Christopher (25) and Nicole (22) Tomasello. He is also survived by his stepchildren from Helen's prior marriage, Dawn Randeals (56), Michael Morgan (54) and his wife Alexandra, and Renee Staten (53) and her husband Marvin. Helen Leahy predeceased him in January of 2011. Danny Leahy passed away in his sleep on Sunday, February 10, 2013. He had just celebrated 45 years of sobriety. A memorial service in his honor will be held on Saturday, March 16, 2013 at 10:00 am, at South West Community

September 1, 2009

<u>To Whom Ever It May Concern:</u>

<u>Subject:</u> Comments about Danny Leahy

I am writing these comments in favor of Danny Leahy because he has crafted or influenced hundreds if not more than a thousand individuals with his efforts to improve there life opportunities. He has never wavered in his task to a better quality of life for individuals who deserved a better life style. I applaud his stepping forward to help others solve their problems and to lift themselves up to a new and greater existence. His compassion impacted humans who had reached a low level and he did his best to provide care for those citizens who lacked the ability to act on their own. Danny had a commitment to help people overcome difficulties and return to a position of progress.

My past experience as a teacher for five (5) years and a Community College Administrator for over thirty three (33) years and a volunteer in community organization for over sixty five (65) years has provided me with the opportunity to meet and observe thousands of individuals and I would put Danny Leahy among the top ten percent (10%) of those individuals who are willing to help others with his time, energy, experience and leadership qualities. Danny is a very warm and personable individual and is an excellent role model.

Joe Iantorno

Dr. Joe Iantorno, EdD

TO WHOM IT MAY CONCERN:

Danny Leahy is a foremost leader in the field of Alcohol Addictive Treatment. He has led the ABC Club as one of the most successful and effective institutions for Alcohol Recovery in California.

He is trustworthy and dependable as a professional in Addiction Treatment.

Sincerely,

James W West M.D.

James W. West, M.D.

BETTY FORD CENTER

Serving Patients, Saving Families

July 20, 2009

Mr. Eddie Hernandez
9 Mount Holyoke
Rancho Mirage, CA 92270

RE: Danny Leahy

Dear Eddie:

Thank you for the opportunity to provide a letter of support on behalf of Danny Leahy. I am both pleased and privileged to do so. I met Danny shortly after moving to the desert over 20 years ago, and have known him in a professional and personal capacity since that time. The exceptional leadership he provided to the ABC Club during his tenure, and the positive impact he continues to have on the local AA community, cannot be over-stated. His efforts need to be recognized and rewarded.

About a year ago the Betty Ford Center was in a position to hire Danny in a patient advocate capacity. It was one of the best decisions we've ever made. Danny is universally loved by the patients, and his knowledge, compassion and commitment is unparalleled. My hope is Danny's past efforts and significant contributions will be acknowledged in the form of a financial package that is worthy of his achievements. He undoubtedly has earned it.

Please contact me if I may be of further assistance.

Sincerely,

Michael S. Neatherton
President

Betty Ford Center at Eisenhower
39000 Bob Hope Drive / Rancho Mirage, California 92270-3297
760-773-4100 / 800-854-9211 Toll Free (U.S. and Canada) / FAX 760-773-4141 / www.**bettyfordcenter**.org

58

Halloween Chemo

St. Patrick's Day Chemo

CHAPTER 12

Interviews

Bill W

My initial interaction with the ABC Club occurred in Oct. 1979 when I was admitted for recovery from alcohol addiction. During this time at the ABC Club I had my first dealings with Danny and Helen Leahy. My first interview with Helen intimidated me. But, I was to learn what a wonderful caring human being Helen was. My relationship with Danny, while not intimidating, was also the same as my feelings about Helen.

After I left ABC I remained in contact with the club as a member of the board of directors, as well as interest in its daily operations. Unfortunately, I found it necessary to once again test the waters; with the result being that I now fully accept the fact that I am an alcoholic. At this point in time I returned to the club for recovery services in July 1987.

Shortly after my return to the club Helen decided to go into treatment for her agoraphobia, and I was asked by Danny to take over the accounting functions. I was also given the grand sounding title of assistant director of the facility. I was to remain at the ABC Club for the next twenty-three years during which time I rose to become the chief financial officer, and to begin my journey of learning about substance abuse and its affects upon people. My mentors in this activity were Danny and Helen. Helen for her part was one of the most compassionate and understanding of people that I had ever had the pleasure to meet.

Not only was Helen very understanding of people, but in her position as program director she was instrumental in establishing the many programs which were instituted at the club. Some of these programs, for instance, were the perinatal program which was one of her favorite programs, but also the many other substance abuse learning programs.

The pregnant women had a nursery in the women's house (The Doll House). How the perinatal program worked was the ABC Club got pregnant girls from the court, and those who came voluntarily. The girls stayed at the club until they had their baby, and generally stayed six months after the baby was born. One of the incentives that the ABC Club offered the pregnant women is that if they maintained a year of sobriety they would be given $2,500 when they completed the year. One of the conditions was that the $2,500, which was donated by an anonymous donor, was that they would not get the money until they moved out of the club. By 1997 eighty drug free babies had been born to women living at the ABC Club.

One of Helen's strong points in dealing with residents was her open door policy. Helen felt that it was important that the residents would feel comfortable in dealing with upper management. Helen's open door policy, simply stated, was that she was always available whenever a resident felt a need, or had a problem which they felt Helen would be able to help them with. Among many of Helen's strong points was her ability to listen, a trait which is extremely valuable in dealing with people who in their past were not listened to.

Now my dealings with Danny were of a different nature. Not only was I the CFO, but I was also responsible to be sure that Danny's administrating skills adhered to the many requirements imposed by the state and county licensing authority. This is not to say that Danny did not deliberately follow the regulations. It strictly was not his strong point. Danny left the administration of the facility in Helen's and my care, and Danny did what he did best; and that was deal with people. Danny had the uncanny ability to see right through you and could tell in a minute if you were trying to run a con job on him. Danny would like to say that one con always recognizes another. His early life experiences taught him much about human nature. Danny's ability to deal with people, both male and female, was not a result of formal education, but rather the school of hard knocks.

One of the great things about working for Danny and Helen was the fact that in most cases they would take into consideration my input in dealing with both administration and dealing with people. My wife and I, who met at the ABC Club, were business related, and did many activities which were of a personal nature. As an example Helen and my wife both loved to go antique shopping and so of course Danny and myself sort of followed along with the necessary ingredient called money. The reason I bring this up is that I was able to have both a personal relationship as well as a business relationship. I was always able to separate my position as it related to work, as well as activities which did not involve the ABC Club.

It is important to note that while I had an excellent relationship with Danny and Helen, especially Danny, there were times when we would have shouting matches over a decision Danny had made which I disagreed with. Needless to say we all knew who won the battles.

One of the most important functions that Danny and I performed was taking residents to court in the hope of convincing the prosecutor and the judge that having the resident remain at the ABC Club rather then go to jail and learn to be a smarter criminal. The duties of going to court was split between Danny and myself with Danny doing the Indio court, and I would do the out of town courts. Danny had an excellent rapport with the local judicial system and seldom did Danny not get what he requested from the courts.

My excursions to the out of town courts was generally successful simply because Danny's and the ABC Club's reputation was spread far and wide. Some of the courts that I appeared in are San Francisco, San Diego, Riverside, Phoenix and Tucson Arizona.

One of the great advantages to taking residents to out of town courts was that you learned a lot. Not only of the individual you were taking to court, but also what may be going on at the ABC Club, which was not readily available on a daily basis. Residents many times are more apt to discuss goings on at the club which you in many cases did not learn about until you were away from the club, on a one on one basis. For some reason residents found it easier to discuss events going on at the ABC Club when they were away from the facility and their fellow residents. Another great advantage was that you were available to develop knowledge of the resident. To better help them.

I was elected as the treasurer for the monthly alumni breakfast which was established to raise funds to assist residents who were lacking in financial resources. The alumni breakfast was responsible for purchasing the food for the breakfast so as not to use food which was purchased for the residents daily meals. As an additional activity I was also the treasurer for the annual barbecue which served the same function as the alumni breakfast except it was an annual affair usually in April. The money raised from the breakfast was also used for the purpose of helping residents with both medical and dental costs. Usually Danny and myself would take those residents needing dental services down to Mexicali, Mexico, where we had a dentist who would make himself available to work on those residents who needed dental work. Dental costs were always significantly less then those in the US and the quality of the dental work was for the most part equal to what they would have received in the US.

During the major holidays like Thanksgiving and Christmas, the club would have turkeys and hams donated. With the donation of the hams and turkeys residents would go to several of the restaurants in the area and get donations of desserts, like pies, and cakes. Marie Calendars was always great for donating pies. The dinners which were put together for the holidays were not only for the residents and their families, but for those neighbors who wished to participate. In many instances people would come in from off the street who were in need of a good meal and they were welcomed and fed.

When the Leahy Community Building was completed, an anonymous donor commissioned a life size bronze statue of Danny and Helen. It cost around $65,000 and was stationed in the entrance of the Leahy building. Helen hated it and Danny could care less. The administration that took over had it put in a closet, and wouldn't surrender it. Danny and Helen's daughter, Rene, took a few men and forced the issue. They moved the statue to Danny and Helen's home. It took six men to carry it. It was in the front yard close to the house.

Metal being at a premium price, the statue was stolen. Later some pieces were found at a recycle center.

In summary, my twenty-three years at the ABC Club also taught me about my alcoholism and what was necessary to me to maintain my sobriety. Needless to say Danny and Helen were a significant part of my whole life over the past twenty-three years that I worked there and helped me know who Bill is.

Rene S

I remember the day my mother brought Danny to our home. I was nine years old, soon to be ten. We lived in Indio, California. My mother followed my grandmother around to the most God forsaken places. Grandma lived next door to us in the Arabian Gardens Trailer Park. Mom was single then, and working in a bar. She was a pretty mean pool player. One day she showed up with this guy. She introduced him as Danny. She said we would be seeing more of him. She was right. They spent more and more time together. We stayed at grandma's in the evenings, a lot. I asked mom where they went to. She said they went to meetings at the ABC Club where Danny lived. As a kid I had no idea what meetings were for. We began to spend time at the 'club.' and it was filled with old men playing dominos, sweeping floors, and doing dishes. I asked Danny what ABC meant and he said, "Always buy Coors," and he laughed. I did not get it, but laughed too. One day a very shaky sick looking old man came into the room. Danny was making him drink coke with honey in it. I asked him why, and he said, "So he does not have seizures." His kindness and patience with this person impressed me. I realized at that moment, what he was doing mattered.

When they announced that they were getting married, I felt it was a good thing. I needed a dad and so did my brother. My two sister's father was still alive and ours was not. I think back now at how crazy Danny was to take on this women with four kids with damaged pasts. My mom was damaged too. A divorced (more than once) and widowed woman. What I did not know then was we were a second chance for him. A do over if you will. I did not know he had been in prison. I did know that he had two other children. I did not know that we gave him a reason to get up in the morning. I did not know that he was overcoming that past one day at a time with a God I do not understand. How this God put this patchwork quilt of a family together, I do not know. I did not know that our forever would be full of recovering, relapsing, suffering alcoholics. My parents loved them all. My mom quit the bar, and begin working for a catering business on the fair grounds in Indio. Danny soon started working for the Young's Catering as well. He drove a catering truck to businesses in town. I did rides along with him and we were great company for each other.

As the youngest, I had nothing better to do than pay attention. I tagged along to the club a lot in the early days. Ran up and down the halls. Became acquainted with the people in recovery. They were funny and loud, some were scary, and some sad. My parents were truly in their element around these people. More and more their time was spent at the club. Danny's responsibilities increased there. There was talk of needing a manager. He became that. The man could not spell, and his reading was worse. So my mother with her seventh grade education became more involved. She would be responsible for creating programs that were designed to heal the whole person. My mother was gifted in the organizational part of the office duties. She could talk on the phone, or in person for hours to another alcoholic. She always managed to get the work done.

As staff became a necessity she became the go between for them with Danny. Tact was not in his vocabulary, and tempers did rise occasionally. Mom would sit back and listen to both sides and state how it was going to be. Sometimes loudly, if Danny did not hear her the first time. He always called her his child bride. And when his bride spoke, most of the time he listened. Somehow they complemented each other. They both had the same middle in common, and were able to apply their own recovery to the problem at hand.

What my parents knew then and believed their whole lives was that if you have one more day of sobriety than the next guy or gal, you matter. You are important and you have work to do. If you were a resident of the ABC Club you held out your hand and lifted that other person up. This was a true peer oriented recovery house. The people that went through those rooms came back to give back. Became staff and board members. Became the fathers and mothers, sons and daughters God intended them to be. They were able to reach their full potential. Residents became lawyers, nurses, policemen and women. They became the alumni of a strengthening force for sobriety.

My parents never lost sight of AA and the steps they took to get where they where. The traditions and meetings of step programs like Al-anon, Alcoholics Anonymous (AA), Narcotics Anonymous

(NA), Alcoholic Children of Alcoholics (ACA, and Co-dependents Anonymous (CODA.), were all offered and mandatory for some. There were parenting classes. Residents were encouraged to go to school. My high school drop-out parents knew the value of an education. If residents were in trouble with the law, Danny showed up in court to vouch for them. They had counseling available to those who chose it. They provided a safe, warm place for people to heal. Plenty of food and stuff to gain strength and wisdom from. The sick fallen down drunk man, or women could now surrender. Now begin a lifelong journey, if they paid attention. If they wanted what the others had and were willing to stay. If they did what was recommended they would heal. Most did. Some died out there. As a kid I remember how upset my parents would become at a death. They took it personally as if they had lost a friend, and they had. Most of the people who went through the house, became friends. My parents never pretended to be better than any of them. They rejoiced in the successes, and cried for the failures. They celebrated babies, and weddings, and cried at funerals.

In the early days it was nothing for me to come home to a strange kid, whose parent was in the 'house.' Nor did I find it odd to have strangers at the dinner table. My parents lived and breathed the ABC Club. Our home phone was connected to the club phone. If no one else could be found to go, to see, and talk to the drunk, off they would go. There were meetings in our home. After meetings at the club mom and the gals would pile around our television to watch Dallas. We lived a few blocks from the club. We were just an extension of it to most.

As the communities need grew so did the club. My parents, the staff, and board members grew it up to encompass women, and women needing to birth sober babies. Transitional housing for a gentle re-entry to the community. At times taking on city hall and the government, insurance companies and the like. They were relentless in this effort. All the while sobering up one drunk at a time one day at a time. They started to get worldwide recognition and awards. None of this mattered to my mom. She was embarrassed by it. "Women of the Year," she would giggle. The Firestone Award did humble them. I think it occurred to them they were special at that point. My mom was very shy really. She suffered from anxiety most of her life. She did not want, nor seek the limelight. Danny was the opposite. He loved being able to promote the recovery center. His life's work. He loved the people loudly. He loved being in the company of movers and shakers in the community. He had earned his place there. He was one. My mom hated the podium and rarely if ever spoke at one. My dad loved the podium, and talked at them often. They were two different people who managed to do amazing things together.

When this story turns tragic is when my mom is diagnosed with lung cancer. Thirty-eight years of doing this deal, and she is given three to six months to live. Still at the helm of the ship she has to retire. The HMO she had paid into will not cover her treatment, or another opinion. She left with sadness the home she had known for forty years. This left Danny to trudge the waters alone. He could not. He made some political errors and it cost him his directorship. He felt betrayed by the very people he had helped sober up. Their wives and families were his own families. The ABC Club Board of Directors felt it necessary to bring in a new man to fill the position my parents had filled all those many years. This move destroyed him. He was never the same again.

While my mother fought her cancer, with the help of amazing women of the program of Alcoholics Anonymous. He went to bed, and stayed there for a year.

The women I will be forever grateful to are Sunny and Gay Hinchey. They took my mother to every chemo appointment. Laughed with her, and cried with her. She did not die after six months. My mother lived another three years. During that time after the year in bed my dad began to reach out. The male members had began to take him by the hand and lead him out of a darkness that almost swallowed him. He started work at the Betty Ford Center. You see he had more experience with the real alcoholic than most ever would. The Betty Ford Center saw the value in that. He began to see value in himself again. Unfortunately most of the decisions made those last two years of my mother's life were based on her illness. She wanted to move to Oregon. Where two of her daughters lived. Danny had to take a leave of absence for the place that had given him a sense of worth again. He began a slow spiral into depression again. Sleeping at all hours. Mismanaging his diabetes. Railing at God for taking my mother first.

When my mother died in the early hours of the morning, it was in a bed that Danny lay right next to her in. The family was there and she was gone. Danny never recovered from her death. The hospital trips became more frequent. He only wanted to be with my mother. We moved him back to Indio. Thinking that being around the familiar men and women he had known and loved for years would help. It did not. He began sleeping a lot again. He had given up. My mother is what he had lived for. The club is what he had lived for. They were now gone, and he could not see his own worth. When I got the call that he had been taken to ICU and put on a ventilator, I cried. He had finally managed to get his own way. I flew to the desert and when I reached the hospital he was sitting up talking to a member of the program. I fell into a false sense that he was too stubborn to die. We arranged for him to go to a rehabilitation center. He was actually doing the exercises. We fixed up his home for his return. After two weeks and his forty-fifth sober birthday celebration with a parade of other members, I felt okay to return home to Oregon. Less than twenty-four hours later I received a call that he was gone.

I was so mad. I yelled to the sky at him. "We were on plan B. You were not suppose to die!" You see I had always thought of him as my father. I had been a little girl and grew up in his shadow. I shared my childhood with the alcoholic. I became one. I too went through the ABC Club. I detoxed in the same room that had been my mother's office in the early days. The foundation I received there made it possible for me to never pick up a drink again. I have my father's maniac in my head. But he always said, "You don't have to act on it." I learned a lot from my parents. We did not always see eye to eye. We fought, we loved, laughed and cried together. I now am that peer reaching my hand out to another suffering alcoholic.

The directorship may have changed at the now called ABC Recovery Center Inc., but my parent's fingerprints are all over the walls of those rooms. Their very souls will dwell there forever. In every recovered alcoholic they will live on. It was a life well lived.

Danny Jr.

I came to the club around the first week of July '95 for four days. That was the first time I had any interaction with my dad, or Helen. Then after the four days I left and went home. I came back down the 21st of July and stayed in the house for eighty-eight days. My dad and Helen weren't around much when I was in the house. I don't know if that was a planned thing, or good thing, or whatever. It was an experience in the house; it was different. The reason I came down here is I had a problem with methamphetamine, and alcohol, and a problem with life, at that point in my life.

After, I left at eighty-eight days, around the first, or second week of October. I came back down for Thanksgiving that year with my son Christopher, my daughter Nicole and my girlfriend at the time, Brenda. Life was just life.

My time at the club I made some pretty good relationships. Met some really good people, and some of them I'm still friends with today.

A Friday night on two separate occasions there were three that were loaded. That was quite an experience that night in the house. Half the house were ticked off. The three were getting loaded and they couldn't, and the other half had anxiety and fear. Them walking around loaded and people trying to stay clean and sober in a clean and sober environment. That was eye opening for myself. I've stayed friends with one of them and over the years, and a couple of times we came back down here and he checked into the club.

I do H&I (hospitals and institutions) at a detox center in San Francisco the second Tuesday of every month. I hadn't seen my friend for five, or seven years, and about three years ago I ran into him there. His whole family were alcoholics. His dad had long time sobriety and his sister is sober today, and he has lost two brothers to this disease. One overdosed and the other one died of complications to his health. I walked up to this center, and in he walked. I hadn't seen him for years. His mom passed away and he inherited a lot of money. For the last seven, or eight months he was on the streets, panhandling for enough money to get a bottle and a dope bag. We stayed in that facility an hour. It was an H&I commitment. Afterwards I talked to my friend about

71

fifteen minutes. I gave him my number and I pleaded with him to call me, but I never heard from him again. It's those kind of things that I remember. I remember the first couple of days in detox when Madd Dog Daze was going on. My dad and somebody else picked up Denny R and brought him back to the club that night. I was fortunate myself, with some other guys to sit around and listen to what he was talking about. It was a real eye opener when I heard what he went out and did. (Denny committed suicide by slashing his neck with a coffee can lid over by the railroad tracks).

I've been around the streets, I was okay growing up, and I've been to funerals for the family. I've witnessed it. Seeing somebody trying to change his life, and then going back to what they were doing, I just couldn't fathom, or realize at the moment.

The relationship with my dad before I got in the club was nonexistent. I'd wanted nothing to do with Helen. Not at first, but after I got to know her better, and she got to know me. I learned to love that lady. She was an amazing part of my life. We would sit and talk about everything. Sometimes we wouldn't talk about anything, we'd sit and watch home improvement TV shows, and antique things. I felt so comfortable around her, like she was my mom. A couple of times I think my dad was, well not resentful but? Me and Helen would tease my dad. We could relate to the same things. My dad had no clue how to pick up a hammer, let alone use a screwdriver. Helen would laugh about that.

About a week before she found out she had cancer, her and my dad stopped, from Oregon, at my house that night. I wished I'd had more time to spend with her. We had dinner together and they spent the night and they were off the next day. Those are the kind of moments I miss. Not being able to spend more quality time with both my dad and Helen. It is what it is, I don't like it but that's just how it is.

Sharon Koski -- Marriage and Family Counselor (non-addicted)

I met Helen through Polly Wentworth when I was a probation officer. Polly was doing some alcoholic and drug work with one of the probationers that I had on my case load. We got talking and I was telling her that I was kind of looking for a place to do some intern work, or just do some volunteer work. We talked about the different areas I'd been trained in. She said, "You know, I know this lady over at the ABC Club, Helen, who has this group on Tuesday, that she does around lunch time, that has to do with women's issues. Why don't you come to a couple of the meetings and see if that will fit what your needs are."

I said, "Well, we also have to make sure that whatever I'm doing is helping. Not standing in the way of people getting clean and sober." So that's how it all happened. Then I went to my first meeting and I was hooked. Helen was gracious, as she always is, and was very open to approaching new ideas. To cover new topics in the group that I was familiar with, like sexual assault, like child abuse and assault, sexual and physical abuse. I was also very familiar with AA and alcohol and drug treatment because in California I had been trained by the Johnson Institute to work with the probationers that I had in California. She thought that was a real nice combination.

I started coming every Tuesday at lunch time and it grew from there, the group, also the size of the group grew as people started coming in, women did that didn't necessarily live in the house. They heard about the group and some of the topics that we were covering. That also led me into, after quite a few years, I said, "Well there has to be something I could do with the male residents."

Helen said, "You know a lot of them have this domestic abuse program their supposed to go to, but they can't afford it, nor can we let them leave the house."

I said, "I ran a program in California, so let me do this. Let me see if I can work something up where I can put together these stages of domestic abuse with the Twelve Steps." I got that all made up in a wheel format. That was the class. We put some paper work together, and a program.

Danny took it over to the court and asked them if this would be acceptable. Here is the therapist, here is her background and this is what she wants to do. So that's how I ended up doing the Anger Management Group for the male residents

I did some other things. Helen and I were a good match because she knew almost instinctively what each of the girls would need. In reference to really have a framework for their recovery. Almost like a mannequin and then you would cloth it. Each mannequin would be clothed differently depending on what the needs were, and who they were. With her instinctual nature and my background in a lot of different clinical areas really added another quality layer to what the overall program was at the club.

I have never worked anyplace since then, or before then, that I felt such a presence, a spiritual presence. Definitely when I was consulting with Helen, not so much with Danny because I didn't have a lot to do with him, or interacting with him because, you know he was old time AA, so talking about being sexually abused as a child, you just need to get over it and get on with your life. Rather than looking at how did that impact the decisions you then made the rest of you lives?

He wasn't a real big supporter of what I was doing so most of my interactions were with Helen. She literally saw the significance to the benefits to somebody's program.

Over time Helen and I became friends. I will always consider her my closest friend on a friendship level, on a emotional level, and on a spiritual level. Even after I moved I would come back to California every couple of years so we could catch up, and it was just like a day hadn't gone by. Going around the house, and chuckle and laugh about things. Then when she got the dogs we'd chuckle and laugh about them. We formed a very strong bond with each other. I know for me it started with a huge respect for her and the work she was doing there, because back then there still was a sexist attitude.

Danny was the head of the place. He ran it so he was the one everyone went to, to make decisions. When in fact Helen was the backbone of that place, and the backbone of the program that started there, and even some of them that are continuing there. I brought in some of the students that I was teaching over at Chapman University to do some intern work there and they started the family program. I think it is still going, since Helen's passing.

She helped me through a real tough time and I personally helped her the same way through her agoraphobia She would always tell me I was instrumental in her learning how to do something more than just stay in the neighborhood, or stay in the house, or when she was at the club, just stay at the club. She was finally to the point were she could drive herself around places. I was quite proud of the fact that I had something to do to help her to be a healthier, whole person rather than still having some things that weren't quite all together. I still almost on a daily basis, think about people who where there and that I worked with because when I do these different groups, and also doing individual counseling sessions with those residents who wanted to sign up, and would come every week. It was individual work with those problems that they didn't want to bring up in the house, or the group, or a meeting.

I'm still doing custody and placement evaluations for family court were I interview the parents, the kids, the teachers, doctors, therapists, relatives, and then make a recommendation to the court about what is in the child's best interest in reference to spending time with each of the parents. Even though I'm not doing clinical work anymore I'm still working for dysfunctional people. It's just like I can't get away from it. I worked eleven and a half years for Dane County, in Madison Wisconsin. I decided it was time for me to retire and just be an old lady sitting on the porch reading her book. But I couldn't stay away from work. Someone would call and say, "I've got this family. Come do this." Milwaukee County needed mediators, and then I started working there. I'm not doing clinical work, but I'm still working with families that are dysfunctional.

My background, a lot of it, was my experience at the club, and has made such a difference in the quality of my rewards. I've been told on several occasion that my work at the recovery home, my work at the Rape Crisis Center, and the training I got in different places have really made the reports for the judges more inclusive, and more detailed. I can only thank every resident that I worked with. For allowing me to be a part of their life, and trusting me with their stories, and be willing to do new things, or at least do old things differently. I can't tell you what a compliment that is to me.

Matter of fact the club with Danny and Helen are still so much in my heart that the last time I was out there Danny took a picture of myself, my partner and Helen. We have that on the mantle of the fireplace in the living room. Helen is with me wherever I go. She was a special, special lady.

Marian Rickert - RN -- Marriage and Family Therapist (Non-addicted)

I went down to ABC, I believe, in '97, it's a recovery center, to apply for an internship working on my masters at Chapman University. Helen Leahy is who I talked to. She said to come on board. Even though I was an Al-Anon, and I was the only Al-Anon on the staff. She welcomed me and I started my internship. I did twenty hours per week. Helping her with groups and seeing people individually, and just seeing how the agency operated. I felt very much at home there even though it was in a rough area of Indio. I had grown up in kind of a rough town so it didn't bother me the least.

When I completed the internship and all the hours. I think it was three-thousand hours. I asked Helen if I could come on as a therapist. It was setting a precedence because they hadn't had a therapist. She said, "Yes." Then in a couple of years we negotiated a decent salary, so I worked there five hours, Tuesday, Thursday, and Friday, five years, or more. I loved the interchange with her. She would sit in on groups, and I was constantly telling her how effectual she was with the women. Helen was so, to me, shy and not very boastful, so she couldn't quite sometimes figure out what I was talking about.

I was telling her how powerful I sensed that she was. I watched the mechanism of the agency, and continued to grow and grow. I went from having an office at the Doll House where I saw clients. Not an office, but a library. When Helen decided to retire after her illness she let me work in her office, which was very, very nice. Then I went over to another office in another building, before I left ABC. I became very attached to her, I think probably she wondered why. I tend to do that sometimes with women. I'm very loyal. I was really loyal to she and Danny as far as the running of the agency went.

I learned an awful lot from her. I still quote varies things that she said. I'm really active in Al-Anon. She often used the expression, "If the person really wants sobriety there's nothing you can do to stop them, and if they don't want it there's nothing you can do to make them want it." I share that a lot in meetings. It really, really helped. A very powerful, insightful statement. I got the impression that she never did realize how powerful she was, but I think that went with the humility of it.

I thought of beauty, she was the prettiest women and she's so gracious and I really loved Helen.

It was my favorite job in the whole world. I call them my little addicts/alcoholics. The people who had issues with abuse, or grief and loss. I learned so much from each one of them. They couldn't believe how I kept close notes. Why did I even care about their past and trauma. That was the way I was taught to do the family model, and you keep notes so you can help them refer back to their childhood trauma. That sort of thing. I got so much experience there. In essence would still be there except you know I was so loyal to Danny and Helen and when the administrative change came they eliminated my position too.

By then Helen had passed. It was really hard to leave there. I would say it was one of the best jobs I'd ever had. My previous jobs were in nursing, which I loved too. In obstetrics, but this one really gave me a chance. I prefer the clinic setting to one on one therapy with people sort of hanging out a shield. I'd rather do the clinic setting. I had heard through the grapevine that probably I would be let go. My husband said he thought the writing was on the wall. I kept thinking, well they will keep the therapist. It didn't turn out that way, so I had to suck it up and leave.

I kept close touch with Helen during her illness, somewhat. Tried not to bug her too much, but people would keep me posted how she was doing. She put up such a valiant fight with the illness.

The clients, I learned so much from her regarding sobriety and what to focus on, so they felt empowered rather than weaker and worse about themselves. She always included codependency in the treatment model. She was open to childhood trauma. In the aspect of addiction she was open. I really felt blessed to be there and to this day when I meet folks out at conventions and such it makes my heart so happy to think I impacted a few of them over there. They have memories and it meant a lot to me.

It was all due to her giving me the opportunity. There really hadn't been such a position in the past. So I really felt that she, she never verbalized it, but it seemed like she really liked me. I appreciate that about her and once I got to appreciate her personality I know she wasn't a talker. But I don't think she ever recognized her power, in reference to decision making.

I joked with her when we got the new building. I said, "Helen, why aren't they moving over there? They won't go over there until the momma bear goes over. Once you go over the rest of them will go over, because treatment centers too are kind of a family model. They're just one big family. They got the mom and dad." Sure enough once she went over everybody else started to migrate over there.

One of my fondest memories is watching her walk from her house over to the center. She just really seemed happy and methodical. I really enjoyed the way she kind of kept herself insulated a little bit. There was so much chaos going on at the treatment center. You would have to develop some kind of technique to not absorb it all. I was always grateful to be part time. Then I had a day or so in-between. I didn't have to concentrate on the sadness all the time. She developed her own skill.

We did get a chance a couple of times to socially be with Danny and Helen and I always enjoyed it. Just the different ABC functions, or I sat with them once at Madd Dog Daze when my husband was gone. I would make her laugh quite a bit. She thought I was pretty funny. I used to marvel at how she kept her sanity inside of such a chaotic place at times.

I can still picture her sitting in the overstuffed chair with her leg up and her little drink. She always had her drink. Just kicking back at the end of the day. I liked that calmness and the residents really, I think, appreciated that. Most of them hadn't had any stability, not much of parenting. They needed that too.

I had a ton of love for Helen. I hope it shows through.

Brandon L (non-addicted son)

Sometimes I share my story, but I am so far removed from it now. People can't fathom that my life was really like what it was. Mom coming home and trimming her weed plants, and putting them in the oven to dry out faster. My step dad Boyd coming home, but stopping for a twelve pack to finish off the drunk he's got going.

What brought me to the ABC Club? My mom showing up for the wrong meeting one night, and realizing that it wasn't the wrong meeting. Shortly after that mom had a grand mal seizure trying to get sober and had met Helen. I remember when she checked into the club I was upset because I couldn't talk to her on the phone. When I finally did talk to her on the phone I had this picture in my head of a very sterile hospital environment. Almost like an institutional quality to it. That was absolutely opposite of what the club was. I wasn't around the club much the first time mom was there. I did go to Ala-Teen Meetings at Fellowship Hall. My initial meeting with Danny I was very intimidated. He was the authority figure of the club to me at that time and that was all I knew about him. Mom was in the club five weeks the first time.

The second time she was there I lived with another resident's son at Danny and Helen's house, while they were on vacation. What I remember about Danny at that time was the final authority on everything at the club. Absolutely just, fair and knowledgeable. He knew what was right and what was wrong and he passed his judgment on it, and that was all there was to it. I was living in the club and I went to the meetings. It was a house rule. I knew if you lived there you had to go to meetings. During the summer I had traveled and stayed with friends here-and-there. They told me I could stay with them permanently, but I didn't want to leave my mother, and I told them no. I had no idea what I was getting myself into. Things were so messed up. My first two weeks at the club I slept in the station wagon. After that I slept on the floor. Then I got my own couch in the big house. That didn't last long and then I was in the front bunkhouse for the rest of the time. Danny also made me do chores. I was a part of the house and everybody had chores to do. It was almost like it was when I was in the military. Everything is structured and you knew what was expected of you.

The hardest part of living at the club was trying to have friends at school. It was difficult. I can remember going to Magic Mountain with some friends and when they were going to drop me off, I wouldn't tell them where I lived. I made them drop me off at a house a couple of doors down. They were doing the good parent thing watching me walk up to the house, and here I was going around the corner to go to a different house.

In the tenth grade my class was having a guest speaker show up, and the guest speaker happened to be my roommate at that time.

Helen I mostly knew when we would be over at her house. She would kind of take care of me. I was in-and-out of the office when she was at work, but I didn't have a lot of interaction with her. That's when it was only the big house and the women's house.

I don't have a desire to drink. I have so much tendency, and personality of addiction, but I don't have the addiction for the substance. Some of the kids I went to Ala-Teen with and hung around with ended up in recovery. I think Danny may have been stricter with me, or I may have followed his directions more. I did participate in the meetings, and I did read the AA Big Book. It has shaped my beliefs and how I see life. I liked to go off walking, or on my bike to Circle K and get a coke and a Snickers bar. I had a roommate and he was a great guy, very intelligent and my buddy. He was sober for a while and doing really good. One time I was walking back from Circle K, and he was drunk and came out of the bushes, and asked me for some money, and I didn't even recognize him. That's when I realized how frightening the addiction could be. Here was this super guy, intelligent and two or three weeks later living in the bushes again.

One guy going thorough detox having the DT's (Delirium Tremors). That definitely shaped my beliefs. One guy having hallucinations in the middle of the night. That was probably my freakiest time. Another guy was hallucinating that the upstairs was on fire, and he was going crazy. Danny Paley, the cook, got up and quieted him down. If anything, seeing how terrible it is, and living in that environment had a lot to do with shaping my beliefs.

Mary E LPN

Where do I start? The first day my husband Ken asked to get in the ABC Club--the state was holding our six kids hostage, the Feds were taking our home and criminal court wanted to put us in prison--Ken went into Danny's office while I sat in the dining room, pregnant and crying. Ken told Danny, "I feel like God has abandoned me."

Danny said, "God ain't abandoned you." And he gave him a bed, actually, a couch. I went and got his stuff. Six months later Danny went to court with us. He asked Ken, "How long have I known you and how many kids have you got?" We told him six months and seven kids. When the judge called our name, Danny got up and said, "I've known these folks a long time and they've got a bunch of kids." The judge gave us probation and community service. Considering we were found guilty of drug manufacturing, that was a miracle.

Ken remained in the ABC Club for another six months. During that time he volunteered to head the Outreach Program and took new residents to tell their stories to kids at the local high schools. I started volunteering too, helping new residents fill out health questionnaires. I had a nurses license but it was in the process of being revoked because of my felony conviction. Danny got me an attorney and paid for a psychiatric evaluation the lawyer said would help. It did, plus the fact that Danny and Helen went to my hearing and asked if I could be of service at ABC. I got to keep my license and to make amends to my profession and my community. I went back to school to become a midwife and public health nurse. I worked at ABC for eighteen years, looking after all the residents, but especially the pregnant women. Danny and Helen even let me deliver babies there for the women who needed a safe and comfortable setting in order to bond with their babies in the best possible way. Those women worked hard to be healthy so they wouldn't need to go to a hospital. My husband Ken ran the Outreach Program for eighteen years and we taught Parenting Class together. Danny and Helen helped us live up to our potential.

When I was pretty new to the club, doing my community service, Danny asked me to take a drive with him. We were gone for almost six hours: I had no idea we were going to visit several sick people. We went to convalescent homes and acute care hospitals. Danny didn't want anyone to feel alone, or forgotten. Later, when one of the residents had a premature baby at the hospital, Danny told the nurses that he was the grandpa in order to visit.

Arlyn Rudolf

I met Danny when Dr. Paul first started the 7 a.m. meeting at Fellowship Hall in May 1980. They used to have a May First party every year, but when I moved away they stopped doing that. One of those mornings was when I first became aware that I was an alcoholic at a very deep level. They didn't have what they have now, which is basically guys from the tracks.

Danny would bring the drunks from the railroad tracks. One morning, at the 7 a.m. meeting, I was all showered, went to the meeting, and sat at the end of the table. Danny brought the guys in and he sat a guy named Eddie next to me. I could not figure out why he would sit Eddie next to me. He looked like he came from the weeds and the tracks. He was running from every orifice, and he stunk to high Heaven. My first feeling was awe why next to me? Something happened, I still don't know to this day how it happened. Somebody called on me and I started to chat away with my share, and all of the sudden I put my arm around him and out of my mouth came, "I just got it, we have the same disease. The only difference between him and me is I didn't drink today." That was my first really deep acknowledgement of my own alcoholism.

Danny came to the meeting every morning. We met at 7 o'clock. Danny was kind of hard on me. It was a matter of time before I realized why he was hard on me. He was hardest on me because of my honest self deception. I don't call it denial. They talk about it at the Betty Ford Center. They call it honest self deception, which I had a lot of. If Danny asked me something, whatever response I gave him, he would tell me I was lying. I had no clue that I was lying. I had to fight for myself, "No I'm not," and on out to the parking lot. Him telling me I was lying and me defending myself. We'd get louder and louder, and I would say, "Everyone can hear you." I was so concerned about everyone hearing me. Those occasions were so important to me.

Some of our fights were because I was trying to get a message across to him. But most of our fights were because I was just trying to agitate him, piss him off. I used to love to do that. Of course he knew I loved him. You don't do that to a person you don't like, you stay away from them. You don't stay away from the people you love.

84

Once I was in Texas seeing my son and I saw this baseball hat with two beaks on it. It said, 'Which Way Did They Go? I'm Barely Here.' I took it back to Danny and he threw it across the room.

He said, "Asshole." Danny was so one of us.

Danny was real. Every time he shared he was just so real. Another way I pissed him off was when Helen had the women's meeting at their house. I used to go to the women's meeting every Thursday night. Danny was trying to get a rose garden going. When I would leave there would be one rose, and I would pick it. Then in the morning at the 7 a.m. meeting he would start after me. He would say, "Damn you, you took my rose." These are the fondest memories.

Danny helped me so much. After the morning meeting I was telling him about Joe, that something was not right, and I went on and on. When I finished he said, "You know Arlyn, you get to be right, or you get to be happy." I've never forgotten that. I don't care now if I'm right. I could see my part because I was fighting for my rights. I don't give a shit any more. It just gets old after awhile.

David, who was a chef, called me and said he would be at the 7 a.m. and would I come. Danny would be giving him his cake. I said, "Oh sure I'll be there." David was a chef and a nudist. He had written an article called The Nude Awakening.

He said, "Oh, by the way they are having the First Annual Nude AA Convention in Colorado in June." He said he called Danny and told him God said that Danny should be the Sunday morning spiritual speaker.

Danny said, "He did not."

At the Roadrunner Meeting at St. Francis of Assisi, we would split up and one bunch would go into a small room and the other stayed in the big room. I went in the smaller room, and when we went back in for the closing announcements, I could see Danny out of the peripheral of my eye. I put up my hand and said, "There is going to be a nudist AA Convention in June, and I have it on very good authority that God asked our very own Danny Leahy to be the Sunday morning spiritual speaker." Everyone just howled.

Danny yelled across the room, "Asshole! He did not." The next morning I arrived at the meeting at Fellowship Hall. Danny always sat with his back to the window, and I sat next to him.

"Good Morning Danny," I said.

He grumpily said, "Good morning." When David called on him to share, he shared, and at the end he shared to the women that he hoped they get a real bitch for a sponsor, and the biggest one was next to him. Those were the good old days when we could make fun of one another. We all cross talked and popped off making fun of one another. It's a different ballgame now.

Renee E

I moved to the desert from Beverly Hills to be editor of a national magazine here. I kept on going up and up in my career. By the time I had ten years sobriety I was fairly successful. My sponsor sort of bought into that. She said because I'd been so good in AA that God was being good to me. I've since found out that God doesn't pay you off. Not with money anyway.

I bought a house in Indian Wells and I knew that there was an Indio, but I didn't know where it was. I knew there was a place called the ABC Club in Indio that low bottom drunks stayed in, and they needed everything from clothes, to furniture. So, I'd call them up and they'd send somebody to pick up my clothes. Once I had a couch that I didn't want anymore and I gave them the couch. That's how I knew about the ABC Club.

However, when I was ten years sober my life just collapsed. I didn't want to drink, I just wanted to die. My sponsor was Arlyn Rudolf who now lives in Palm Springs, she said, "Lets go talk to Helen and Danny. Because when Helen was eleven years sober she went into a recovery home called Meta House. Her life wasn't going the way she wanted it to. She understands that you can break your commitments to a Twelve Step program, without going out drinking, or eating, whatever it was."

So I went to their house with Arlyn. Arlyn said, "Tell them your story." So I did. I was going to lose my house because the company, the agency, I started that had the windmill industry as a major client was pulling out. The other clients that I had were not enough to sustain me. I was losing my business, I was losing my house, and I was losing my boyfriend. I was just nuts. But I didn't want to drink. Danny said, "Listen, I don't have a room for you, but if you want to come, you can come and sleep on the couch."

I said, "Okay."

So I went into the ABC Club. I was not prepared for that. You have to remember I'm a Jewish American Princess. I had been very well educated and had been quite successful in business. I got to the club and they'd say, 'She has ten years sobriety? I'd cut my wrists if I was like that with ten years sobriety,' or they would say, 'she doesn't have ten years sobriety.' They were not easy with me. In retrospect I don't think I was an easy person, because I thought an awful lot of myself. I like to think I was honed at the ABC Club. Just like two rocks that rub against each other, and smooth each other out. I got smoothed out and I knew I couldn't depend upon my education, my money, or anything except my ability to live this program. To think I was a worthwhile human being.

I switched everything. I switched from being in the business world, to going into bilingual education. When I left the club I taught sixth grade in Thermal as a bilingual teacher because I knew Spanish. I had learned it in Puerto Rico. I did not learn it from my family of origin. My family of origin is East Europe Jewish. My Spanish is very good.

Anyway, I slept on the couch and I went to meetings and did everything. One day about five days later I woke up and said, "I know this couch. This is the couch that I donated." That was a good way of cutting me down to size.

I'm really a skeptic at heart and I have not met that many people who I am wild about, and I was wild about Danny. After some years he hired me to do a group. I have a counselor license in alcohol and drugs. He hired me to do the Aftercare Group. It was wonderful. It was every Wednesday night, and not much money, but it was lovely.

I hung around the ABC Club a bit. Several times I was in the outer office, of Danny's office, doing something or other, and he was on the phone inside his office. I would hear him talking to a mother, or a father who was telling him about their child being in jail. He was in the midst of all kinds of things. There was always something happening at the ABC Club. He would say, "Okay, I'll meet you at the courthouse in forty-five minutes." He'd hang up, get up, go to his car and go over there, and bring the boy back. Usually it was a boy who was going to be in jail. I'd see him do this over and over again, and bringing people into the club that needed to be in jail. There was never a question of, do you, or do you not have money. He never asked me for money, although I had made a lot of money. Of course I also had spent a lot of money. That's the way he was. He really was into saving lives.

Then he was one of those people, especially because he stuttered, that was very easily thought little of. He was enormous. His sense of ethics was good. He never learned how to charm people one-on-one.

He'd go around calling people assholes with the greatest affection. He'd say what's on his mind to you. That's one of the things he did, but he did it beautifully. He used to have this Pack Your Shit Meeting. He'd find out that somebody had screwed up in one way, or another and he'd just tell them, "Go pack your shit and get out." They would.

There are other ways of doing this, but that wasn't Danny's way. But with that harshness came a caring that was extremely profound.

A strange thing happened. There was one of those Joe and Charlie things (they opine AA books), but it wasn't them. It was to be a group at the ABC Club. I went to find out when and how I could go, only to find out they were sold out. So I went into Danny's office and there was Danny, and he was cleaning out around his office, so I asked him if he could do something because I wanted to go to this Joe and Charlie group. He told me not to worry, that he would. Of course, he did. But he was cleaning up his office, and there was a lot of stuff all over the place. I don't know why but as I was leaving I turned around and said, "You know, you are one of the few best people I know." I don't know why I said that.

He said, "Oh, you know I'm an asshole." I found out later he was packing up his office because he was told to leave. The fact that I had said that at that moment was really important.

I didn't know how sick he was. The last time I saw him at an ABC Friday night meeting he had shaved his beard and I barely recognized him. And then I heard he had died. His memorial meeting was stupendous. There were so many people there, so many people touched by him. I had just come, a few weeks before, to a really important man's memorial, a doctor, and he was a major contributor to AA. I did not feel the absolute total admiration for him as I felt at Danny's. I'm a compulsive overeater and I was so touched at Danny's memorial I could go out and eat. The man deserves a place in AA History like no one else. He is such an indication that you can not judge someone by the amount of education they have, or by the way they speak. He was just full of care and love. Nothing was too much for him to do. He took me into the ABC Club when I was not drinking, I was not using. I was just falling apart.

I stayed for two, or three months. I was ready to leave and walked out of the old house and I twisted my foot, and fell, and I couldn't walk. I had to go around in a wheel chair and ask people to drive me. Danny said God was doing for me what I couldn't do for myself. Danny was a fabulous man and he will be sorely missed. I was in love with Danny, so Helen didn't like me very much. I never made a play for him, or anything like that. I was in love with him, and she really didn't trust me.

Gary P

I arrived at the ABC Club September 23, 1994 from jail. I was very happy to finally be out of jail and was willing to do whatever to stay out. I had, for the first time in my life, asked for help while in jail, and was taken into the Second Chance Program on June 16, 1994. That was the last day I put any kind of mind altering substance in my body. My sobriety date is June 17, 1994.

On the second day at the club is when I met Danny Leahy. The first thing he ever said to me is, "How you doing?" I said, very energetically, that I was doing great, and that life was great. He immediately said to me, "Slow down asshole, life ain't a bowl of peaches and cream," and he turned around and walked away. I was flabbergasted and a little upset. I did not know why he would talk to me like that, but now I do. I did not know what he meant by that, but I learned very quickly and realized he was right.

I began paying attention, and listening to him, and watching him, and what he did. I then met Helen in a group and she told me that if I wanted to change my life I had to start by making the first move, and that it did not matter how small the first change I made was, it would start the ball rolling. So I made what I considered a small insignificant change, and she was right, my life began to change.

Neither one of them ever lied to me, no matter how angry I got, or painful the truth was. I begin working in the kitchen as a cook helper and Danny began to pay more attention to me, and what I was doing. We begin to spend more time together. He would take me with him when he went shopping, and he would talk to me about life and how to deal with it. I started going to his home where I began getting to know Helen.

I felt special when Danny and I were at the swap meet, and Danny introduced me to somebody as his son. Danny quickly pointed out to me that my grandmother was a liar, and that I was not special. I spent a lot of time with both Danny and Helen. Mostly Danny, of course. After I moved out of the club and still spent a lot of time with Danny people would ask me if he was my sponsor. At four years sober I asked him to officially become my sponsor. He remained my sponsor until the day he died.

When my mother passed on Helen stepped in and became my surrogate mother, and helped me with a lot of things that Danny could not. Between Danny and Helen's patience, and tolerance, and love, and the program of AA I was able to stay out of jail and change my life.

At an awards dinner for Danny and Helen I said to him that if I could only, one day be half the man he was, I would be twice the man I am. He looked at me and said, "You are just fine the way you are." Then told me to, "Go sit down, asshole." They became more like parents to me than my parents had been. I loved my mom and dad, but was never able to connect with them, or talk to them about things I could with both Danny and Helen. For the last five years of Helen's life I was honored to take her to dinner on Mother's Day.

All in all, choosing to go to the ABC Club when I got out of jail, and the fact that Danny and Helen were there, I believe, was all my Higher Power's doing. I truly believe that had all not been the way it was, I may not still be sober nineteen years later. They were both instrumental in my sobriety, and still are to this day. I watched Danny always have a sponsor, and when he passed away I did not know how I was going to replace him and a friend pointed out to me that I was not replacing him I was doing what he taught me to do by example, which is how he taught me an awful lot of things. They will always be in my heart, and my sobriety.

There is still a lot to say about Danny and my friendship, but I really don't know how to do it simply because our relationship was not simple.

Russell J

I was living underneath a set of steps behind the Hair of the Dog in Palm Springs, and had been on the streets, sleeping in the dirt, for about two and a half years. I never expected to live in the desert. I'd already had one experience with living in the desert in Arizona back in the early 70s. Didn't like the heat, so I had left, and continued doing what I was doing, and I ended up here mid-October in '84. Basically lived on the streets until I ended up in the ABC Club March 26, 1987.

I had left a job in Wyoming and was on my way to Hawaii to collect Food Stamps and live on the beach all winter long. Then I would go back to Wyoming. It was too cold in Wyoming in mid-October. Unfortunately, or fortunately I ended up here.

As Danny said, "Things happen as they are supposed to happen."

We, me and my friend, had waited for the last check to catch up with us, by the time the check caught up with us, we had drank up all the money we did have. We didn't have enough money to go to Hawaii. My friend did go through the house, but I know he went back out. Last time I saw him was maybe eight years ago. He was living on the streets, in the summer, in Palm Springs.

I was arrested several times in Palm Springs for public drunk. Never once did the judge, or anyone say I had a drinking problem. I didn't know I had a drinking problem. I thought that's just the way it was. I had a friend in New Mexico. About once every six months he'd go to Santa Fe to do what he called, get a 'tune-up' and come back. He'd be okay for five, six months, then go back to Santa Fe and get another tune-up. Toward the end of my drinking when I was literally living in the dirt I thought if I could just go get a tune-up and be able to get a job I'd be able to get the heck out of the desert here and be all right. Unfortunately it didn't happen the way I thought it was going to be.

About four months before I got put in the ABC Club I met a gentleman by the name of Leo. He came by and told me his name was Leo, and he was an alcoholic/addict, and he found a different way to live. He made a habit of coming by every two to three weeks, to see how I was doing. Sometimes he'd give me a bit of work. He had a little construction company.

Every time when Leo went to leave he had a statement and would say, "I'm an alcoholic/addict and I've found a different way to live." Then he made the most profound statement I'd ever heard. He said, "If you ever need me, here's my number, call me." So at 2 o'clock in the morning when I was on a real drunk I called him up. He told me, "Don't ever call me at that time of the night. If you want help you'll call me tomorrow morning." I woke up the next morning with a terrible hangover, and the shakes, and jitters, from getting drunk. I realized that I had made a terrible mistake. I didn't know what would happen, and that I should have never done that. I didn't see Leo for a couple of weeks. One day I was at a place called 'Poke's Bar and Grill' in Palm Springs, insanely drunk again.

Leo showed up and he opened the door of his car and said, "Get in." I just got in. I didn't ask him where, or why.

Next thing I know, he's taking me to a recovery home. We went to the Ranch first, but they didn't have any room at the Ranch, so he took me to the ABC Club. I had no idea where the ABC Club was. I didn't know anything about Alcoholics Anonymous. Leo said I had to talk to this guy named Danny. I walked in the ABC Club and sat down, and Danny goes, "Wawawawhat's your ppproblem?"

I told him, "I think I'm addicted to alcohol."

He said, "I don't have any room."

I said, "Well I'm a Marine and I can sleep on the floor."

Danny said, "Just shut up and go sit down."

So I went outside and sat down. It was on a Friday night, March 27th 1987. Little Jimmy English, a former horse jockey, when it was about suppertime, went and got me a plate of food. I ate and went back and sat down in a chair on the corner, and passed out sitting up in the chair. At that time they used to have a speaker meeting on Friday night. The only thing I could hear as I was waking up, close to the end of the meeting, was this guy saying all he ever wanted to be was a Hell's Angel. It just didn't work out, but he found sobriety instead.

I woke up as everybody was leaving. They put me behind the couch underneath one of the tables, to sleep on the floor in the old house. Next thing I knew it was morning and at that time they had morning meetings on Saturdays. There were five, or six people sitting around a table, and they were going around introducing themselves, saying their name. I just followed their lead. It was the first time I ever said that, "I'm Russell, and I'm an alcoholic," without reservation.

I was so afraid when I was in the ABC Club that people would find out who I was and they'd kick me out. I was afraid they'd do a background check and find out that I'd been arrested many times. I didn't have a prison record, but I had an arrest record. I was totally mortified. The residents in the house told me, "We don't care what your past is. All we care about is what you're doing here."

So that first day (my sobriety date) March 27th '87 they put me at the car wash. I had to go wash cars on Monroe and Hwy 111. I wasn't feeling to good, but I still washed cars. I had a pair of pants with the butt ripped out, and a pair of biker boots. I thought I was God's own drunk, a fearless man.

Danny came by about mid-afternoon and he goes, "How are ya feeling?"

I said, "I'm feeling alright."

He said, "Don't get too well too quick."

About four days later he called me in the office and told me the rules of the house. The most important one being, "Don't leave the property. If you do just keep on going. If you want to get sober, this is the place that will get you sober." I started the process right then learning the principals of AA way of life. The first thirty days no phone calls. Nobody wanted to call me anyway, because I had no friends. I had no family. All I had was me, except my friend who brought some clothes down after I'd been there a couple of days. Of course he had stashed a couple of joints in one of the pockets. They used to go through all the clothes. They found those things, and immediately relieved me of my marijuana.

It was intense meetings. We had a group meeting in the morning, a group in the afternoon, a meeting at night. Every day for a month I sat there and listened to what everybody had to say. I was insanely jealous when other people would get up and say, I've got two weeks, or I've got thirty days. How could anyone stay sober that long? I wanted to be just like them.

Danny took me to Social Services and got me signed up for Food Stamps, so the house could take the Food Stamps and use them for groceries. He told me I didn't have to worry about paying for anything. That the important thing was that I get sober, and try to work the AA principals in my life. The first thirty days I did exactly what they told me to do. I was completely lost. I didn't know where I was at. It took me about three months to figure out exactly where the ABC Club was in Indio. I thought Indio Boulevard was Hwy 111. Yet, when I'd go with Tim and the guys to Fellowship Hall to the Saturday Night Speaker Meeting I was confused as to what was where.

After my thirty were up Danny let me start doing some day labor. I started doing some jobs for the Leo that brought me in. I met one of my best friends, Joe W in the house. He and I would catch the bus on Indio Boulevard and ride into Palm Desert and do some work. We put bathrooms in Fellowship Hall, and the block walls. I totally immersed myself into the AA way of life. Slowly, but surely.

Danny would always have something, I thought was profound, to say to me. He would take me over to the Indio Fashion Mall and buy me frozen yogurt. We sat in the courtyard there and he would tell me different things about living life the way life should be lived. He told me as long as I didn't drink even if my butt was falling off, and go to AA I'd be okay. I had no where else to go. All I know is that when I went to the ABC Club I was sick and tired of being sick and tired of where I was at, and never having anything. I was completely physically, and mentally, and morally bankrupt. I couldn't get enough to eat. I couldn't get enough sleep.

The people at the ABC Club got me clothes, they outfitted me. I had a Datsun F210 when I got to the club. It had to be pushed to start it. The first convention I went to was on a Friday night when Danny said, "Come on I'm going to take you to the Ramada."

When we walked in there must have been twenty pretty ladies standing there all saying, "Welcome." I was amazed. Saturday some of us went back in that Datsun 210 and it stalled on Fairway and Cook. Trying to get it started the cops pulled up behind us, but they let us go on our way. We had to push it at the convention to get it started to get home.

I ended up spending eight and a half months in the ABC Club. I went to all the group sessions that I could, when I wasn't working. Went through some big changes. I'd been working for Leo almost every day, and he wasn't paying me. I told Danny I didn't know what I was going to do. Danny said, "You'll figure it out," and sure enough it got figured out for me because Leo just let me go. Claimed I wasn't working for him. That was okay too.

I went to work for another contractor in the club. Got a good solid foundation underneath me with Alcoholic's Anonymous. I didn't have any extending things to distract me. No family. I'd forsaken my family. Danny told me that my family will be taken care of later, when you're ready to get it taken care of. Danny helped me a lot. In my photo album I didn't have photos until I got sober. The first picture in the album is a five by seven of Danny Leahy. He saved my life.

I got out of the ABC Club, after eight and a half months, I still used to go back for five, or six months and take care of my weekly duties. I had to do cups on Tuesday night, or Wednesday night, and had to spend time in the office. I got involved with the Madd Dog Daze Convention set up, and clean up committee. Danny got me into that. I thought it was wonderful. Somebody finally asked me to do something. I moved into a place in Cathedral City with two other sober members, and worked with one of the sober members, for about a year, for a sober contractor.

I kept going back to the ABC Club. I went through a few mental anguishing moments falling in love, and getting married, and having that fall apart on my one year birthday. Danny told me he was going to write on a piece of paper what would happen. That he would put it in an envelope, and when it falls apart to take it out and read it.

Both of the people that were instrumental in my early sobriety couldn't stay sober themselves. We buried both of them.

I've been active in AA since then. I got married in AA. I married an Al-Anon. I met her at the ABC Club. I thought she had lots of money. She thought I had lots of money. I'm happy with my life, and in love with my wife.

If it hadn't been for Danny and the ABC Club I don't know what would of happened. Danny told me that was just the way it should be.

Freda A

I had been in jail. Through drinking and using drugs I'd gotten into some trouble. I kept relapsing. I'd go to jail and then when I got out I would do okay for a while and then I would relapse again and get in more trouble. This one time the probation officer had a woman with him, another probation officer. She suggested that I find a recovery home that took people for a long term, like a year. I asked around at the jail, like at the little AA Meetings they had in there, and a church group, and someone had given me the address for the ABC Club.

I started writing there, and Michelle R was answering my letters. I told them what my story was and she said I had to write every week. I wrote that I think I'm an alcoholic and I need long term treatment. They put me on a waiting list and I wrote once a week while I was still incarcerated. It was a miracle because they were holding over my sentencing to prison. My public defender stretched out my time until a recovery home had a bed available. A couple of them did, and the judge said, "No!" I received a letter from Michelle R that a bed had become open. On Monday I received that letter, and Tuesday was my next time to go to court and they were going to sentence me. In that little window of time my public defender got a minute order to have me released in the custody of his secretary who would take me straight to the ABC Club. No stopping in between; from Banning Road Camp. It was a miracle.

As soon as I got there I had my little jail box and the clothes I had on. The secretary took me into the office and she told me the director there told her not to stop anywhere. So she delivered me there. I was sitting there nervous with my little jail box thinking 'Oh my God what have I got myself into?' It was hot, already into the end of April. I was from Hemet and it was hot, but not as hot as Indio. The guys had pretty much short haircuts, and shaved. I thought 'I've got myself into some kind of a cult.' Later I found out different. Helen and Michelle were sitting in the office, and there were people coming and going all the time.

After a while Danny came out of his little office in the back. He was looking at me and he said, "You been in jail. Right?"

I said, "Yes."

He asked me directly, "Do you think you're an alcoholic?"

I said, "I think I am."

He said, "Well, you know you never have to drink again. Just follow directions."

Helen just sat in her chair and let him do his thing. Through the years, that's how we did it with Danny. Let him take the rein. I stayed in house, in the Doll House upstairs in room 1. I stayed ninety days in residential treatment. I went from the Doll House over to the Transition House and they let me have a little part time job. A couple of hours three, or four days a week. Sometimes six hours, but they would get all over me, 'your working too much.' I'd come back and do the meetings in the evening. After ninety days I got a little scared. It was time to go to sober living. You don't know. If I'm not going to be accountable to anyone, am I going to stay sober?

They had the sober living houses set up, where we were paying our rent directly to Danny and Helen. So we were responsible to them. We each had a room. This house was a HUD house on Sirocco out in the community. Susanne, Michelle and her little girl, and myself, and another girl had her two children with her. It worked out pretty good. It was not too far from the club, so I could ride my bike over, and pay my rent, and go to meetings. We were required to go to meetings while we lived there. If they didn't see you at enough meetings they were over knocking on the door finding out 'what is going on ?'It was good. We ran the house like the ABC Club was ran. Anytime any problems would come up, Danny and Helen would come over and help iron out the wrinkles. Sometimes we don't get along with other people. As soon as we let them know we were having problems they were right there to help sort through it. Everything they taught us in treatment can be used in life. So every time problems come up, I'm like, 'Okay, I know how to handle this.'

I was in the sober living house for nine months, so it was a total of one year. Ninety days in residential treatment, and nine months in sober living.

I had a little job out in the community at Jensen's Grocery, and my sponsor said, "Freda there's an opening at the ABC Club for a House Mother. I think you would be good for that."

I said, "Oh me." She said because of HUD they were closing down the four sober living houses. It seemed like a good idea because I could live there and still be in recovery, and have a job. So I became the House Mother of the Doll House. It worked out really well. I lived in the House Mother's room downstairs for three years. When I took the job, I worked evenings from 3:00 p.m. to 11:00 p.m. so it gave me time to go to school in the morning, or on my days off. I worked weekends and then had two days off during the week.

My major is Marriage and Family Therapist. I will graduate 2014. I'll be sixteen years sober March 9th. Everything they taught me, because I work in treatment now, I use. And all the little things that Danny would say like, "What she thinks of you is none of your business." I use that stuff today, and it is so helpful. Helen with all her wisdom, and co-dependency. All the time I worked at ABC from March 1999 to 2008 I did the CODA Group once a week. All of that knowledge is really helpful. It's been passed on. All of that wisdom and knowledge that have saved thousands of people. We all grew up in this family that started at the ABC Club.

Danny and Helen ran the house on the principals of the Twelve Steps, and when we run our lives that way it works out really well.

When I lived in sober living, my sponsor Maggie sponsored Margo and I would be at the club at meetings all the time. So Margo got sober, and she was going to meetings. Her brother started coming to meetings. Margo and I were connected through the same sponsor and she introduced me to her brother. I was seeing someone at the time. I thought her brother was cute. He was quiet and kept to himself. Things didn't work out with my relationship. Margo asked me if I was seeing anyone, and I told her no. She asked if I would be interested in her brother and he and I have been together ever since.

Shannon G

I was homeless for three years after my husband died. I had, finally, no where to go and no money. I called my mom, Gay Henchey, and she put me in Hacienda Woman's Recovery in Desert Hot Springs. I stayed there for sixty days. I went into sober living there, but that didn't work out, and I didn't have anywhere to go after that. My mom called Danny, and asked Danny if he could help me.

Danny said he would find a place for me. He found a place for me in sober living. I was there for a year. I'm very grateful for that.

My interactions with Danny and Helen were not a lot. I was uncomfortable around them. My mom was really close to Helen and I thought of her as untouchable. Danny, I was just uncomfortable. I felt that my mom got me a favor with these people and I was afraid of them. Being afraid of them changed, but being uncomfortable, no. I just kept them on a pedestal, so I didn't interact with them much.

I was uncomfortable because I thought my mom had everybody watching me. I was uncomfortable because I thought everybody was judging me at the ABC Club. That was my perception of what was going on.

I am very grateful for the club. I needed direction for a really long time. I thought sober living gave too much freedom, so I needed a little more constructive time. I was glad I had a place to go and a place to live. They took very good care of you. I had lots of meetings and lots of people to talk to. I had lots of groups. I think it was one of the best things that ever happened to me; having the club being available to me. That Danny would allow me to come into the club and be there, and be a part of, was awesome. Very awesome.

I was there a year, and then I moved in with my mom for two years. That was hard. I never had much of a relationship with my mom. The last relationship I had with her I was sixteen, so that was hard. That was the first time she was able to be my mother. It was uncomfortable because she was on me twenty-four, seven. She was always examining me, talking to me, and wouldn't let me be alone in the house. She was always wondering if I was up, when I was coming out, where I was going, what was I doing, always hovering over me. It was really uncomfortable. To have my mom be a mom that I'd never had before. It was hard to accept.

I didn't feel really like family because of our distance with each other. So it was hard. It was hard being her daughter. I was uncomfortable most of the time. I didn't think we had a relationship until she died. (July 2012 Gay Henchey was hit by a car and died as a result of her injuries).

I had one particularly bad experience at the club. I had roommates and there was a lady that did the aftercare group. Her name was Diana I lived right across the street from the office. Apparently I'd come home one afternoon, and a guy that used to be in the club stopped and talked to me before I went in. I said hi and I was glad to see him, and tried to get him to come back. To stay around for meetings and stuff. I don't think Diana saw him leave, so she called Danny and told him I had men in my apartment (the bungalows).

There was a guy visiting that had been there before I got there. He was visiting my roommate. I went in and took a shower and I heard Danny screaming through the apartment. "Where's Shannon, where's Shannon? I need to talk to Shannon. What room is Shannon in?"

I had just gotten out of the shower in my room. I grabbed my robe and I put it on. I said, "Here I am Danny. What do you want?"

He said, "I heard there's a guy in here that doesn't belong here."

I said, "No. You can look, I mean I don't care." I didn't have guys in my apartment. I didn't even date guys. It was really traumatic. I even asked Diana after that and she swore she never did that. I know she did. That was the only bad thing that ever happened. Danny calmed down once he saw that there was nobody there. He threw out my roommate's boyfriend.

I loved living there. They were nice apartments, and close to meetings. I never did understand why they didn't put the pregnant women, or the women with families in the bungalows. Instead of keeping them in the little shacks (the hotel rooms). I thought if anybody needed the bungalows, it was them. The rest of us could stay in the one room, two bed little shacks.

Mary A

When I first got out here to the desert; my parents had brought me out. I was doing some drinking, but not a lot of drinking, but a lot of using. I was out there. I was not a functional alcoholic/addict at all. I didn't know it in words at the time, but as I got into my recovery, some of the expressions, the terminology that I was learning described the point in my life I had got to, I was sick and tired of being sick and tired. I got to the point that I was more scared of what had become familiar then I was some sort of change. I had no clue that I could have changed. I had really hit a bottom in every way.

I called my father who had been involved in Alcoholics Anonymous for at least ten years. I was giving up, surrendering, of course at the time I didn't know that that was what it was. It was the first time that I admitted that I had some problems. I admitted to my dad. He said you accept us helping you not on your terms, and if I didn't want to do that, 'good luck in life.' That was an eye-opener. I knew how hard it must have been for him to say that. I also knew that I better take it while I can. I moved in with my sister who was four and a half years younger than me. She lived here in the desert and was trying to finish up the Nursing Program at College of the Desert. So I lived at her place with my son Garrett who was eight and a half years old. She was trying to get sober and clean herself. Then we stayed with another lady, who was sober and had been in the program for awhile.

During that time I had started going to meetings. Then I ended up on a daytime contract at the ABC Club, going during the day. Attending groups and attending meetings. I was even given a chore. I wasn't even living there yet. I had to clean the windows at the women's house, which was a little house that housed seven women and the house mother. We had a dorm room, and we all had to share one bathroom which could sometimes be pretty interesting. I didn't do things like chores. So I would clean a window and then go sit down and have a cigarette, then I'd go back and clean another window and go sit down, and have a cigarette, and some coffee. I couldn't even focus on doing one chore all the way through. At the time it was the best I could do.

Just in the process of being in the groups I started being able to absorb everything I was hearing. Then I was able to move into the ABC Club and become a full time resident. That was the hardest thing to do, but it was the best thing I was able to do for myself in my whole life. I had to have my son put in foster care and that part was scary. There were some different experiences involving that. My whole time living there was eighteen months.

During that time a lot of the things I saw and heard from other people, as well as the groups and meetings really made an impression on me. Not just people who had come in and then gone out drinking and using again, and coming back, or never coming back. Getting to know people who had gotten sober and clean. Getting to know them in meetings and groups. And some went out again, and died, and they made an impression on me.

The first time I met Danny and Helen was the first meeting I went to at the ABC Club. It was the Friday Night Speaker Meeting. Back then after the meeting everybody would go to Bob's Big Boy, or Denny's restaurant. They would have a meeting after the meeting. I remember meeting Helen and finding out some of her life's experiences paralleled mine. I was really surprised. Danny I didn't know who he was. I didn't realize at first that he was the ABC Club Director. My first impression of him, sitting a couple of tables over, was that he was an older man that stuttered a lot.

I think I learned a lot of things just learning to be present. In between the groups during the day and the meals, I liked to go hang out in the office. To be there near the people. Danny and Helen and some of the staff members, and you, and some of the women I was meeting in the groups. My first memories of you, Sunny, was in the Women's Meeting, and you shared that you were unemployable. I'd never heard that before and I thought 'that's me'. Realizing that when I was drinking and using I was unemployable. I had a few jobs here and there, but I could never keep a job long. I look at it now and realize that the jobs interfered with my drinking and using, and what I wanted to do. I'd always end up quitting or getting fired. I was floating through life.

One of the things that made a big impression on me was when Helen, after she had been sober for a few years, had some issues. She went into a recovery home for herself. That's what she needed to do and not drink, no matter what. That is one of the things I admired about her. She had to do what she did to take care of herself. There were things throughout my sobriety shared about that I could relate to. I learned a lot about myself and my disease. My drug of choice was methamphetamine. Helen had taken courses at a local college so she could do her job better at the ABC Club. From her I learned a lot of stuff about different drugs. How it affects people. Long term results and things like that.

When I left the club after eighteen months I got my first little apartment that was a few blocks away from the ABC Club. I could walk there during the day for the meetings. A week after I moved in to the apartment I got my son out of foster care. I was learning how to parent again. There was a lot of stuff that I was not there for my son. Instead of beating myself up for it I change it, one day at a time. There were a few rough spots that we hit. He was ten years old then. I begin to see some patterns with me and him, and I now had the tools to change that. My son is thirty-five years old now. I realize now that things could have very well gone in the opposite direction. The way things were the first nine years of his life. I know my change and him being around the ABC Club that we have a phenomenal relationship now. If it hadn't been for the club, we wouldn't have that relationship today. I wouldn't have the life I have today. I've had the same job now for nineteen years. I work for a grocery store. I may have had that job at different stores in the chain, but for the same company. That never would have happened. I couldn't even hold a job for a few months, before I got clean and sober. Now I've worked consistently for all those years. Now I get up, and show up, and do my job. I have friends and acquaintances at work. I pay my rent, I pay my bills. None of that was going on in my life before I ended up at the ABC Club. I was able to really be there for my stepmother and dad when they passed away.

Then I met, in meetings, and married Michael, and we were together thirteen years. Some of his illness was a result of his drinking and using. He passed away in September 2009. All the things I've gone through in life I never had to pick up a drug, or a drink, or run away. I learned how to face the things life dealt me. I live life on life's terms. I get through that stuff and I don't have to feel guilty that I could have done this, or I could have done that. My life is good. If I'd been told my life would be like this back then, I wouldn't have believed it. It's not like going from rags to riches, because I'm not rich money wise, or have a fancy car. But I'm rich in my heart, in my life, and in my soul thanks to Alcoholics Anonymous and knowing the people in my life. And knowing Danny and Helen Leahy. I know that I don't have to get caught up in all the negativity. No matter what happens in my life, the mistakes I make along the way I can correct. I know I can stay sober and clean under any and all conditions. My life is good and I am happy with my life.

Andrea C

I was sentenced to do ninety days in county jail in Indio. Three days prior to that I had checked into the ABC Club. The year was 2000, and just before the judge laid down the gavel, the small man with a clean white beard shot up from the audience in the court room. He stuttered but spoke loud enough for the judge to hear him. "Sh sh sh she's with me."

To which the judge responded, "Mr. Leahy, so good to see you."

Then the judge looked at me and asked, "Are you with the attorney, or Mr. Leahy?" I choose Danny. That was the first good decision I had made in many years. I was sentenced to serve the ninety days at the ABC Club in Indio.

Danny took me to have some frozen yogurt and told me not to tell the other residents, "'Cause they will all want some." That's when it all began. "Stay away from the men, get a sponsor, do your steps, you are not a bad person, you have a disease, you can get better, follow the rules, everything is going to be okay."

Nobody wanted me, and nobody trusted me. Everything had been my fault for so long. It was so kind and touched my spirit that was so close to being dead. I stayed clean for two years that first time.

I was in a relationship and we both started using. This relapse lasted till 2004. I came back at about one hundred and ten pounds, and strung out. My teeth were missing and I was pregnant. My dad didn't know how to help me but he remembered I had a good run with Danny, so he called Danny and took me to the club for round two.

Danny never judged me even though the shame of using while I was pregnant was killing my soul. Helen took us girls on women's luncheons where she taught us all about how boundaries are acceptable and will save my life. And I don't have to do things to keep you happy. I have the right to say no, or not now. I have the freedom of saying I don't know, I'm not perfect. I am a women learning to be who I want to be instead of trying to be what you decided I have to be. To be honest to my soul saved my life. I am forever grateful for lunches with Helen. After being clean for two years I ended a bad relationship because of things Helen had taught me. I came back to talk to Danny. I still had nowhere to live.

Helen told me to grab my clothes and my daughter, and come to the sober living house. It was called the McGovern House. They allowed me and my child back to sober living so we could be safe, and honor the boundaries she had so lovingly taught me. I stayed in meetings at the club until Danny no longer ran the place.

I am still clean. I go to meetings in the lower desert area. I have eight years now and have a great relationship with my college student son, my eight-year old little girl, and my year-old twins. I am married and so grateful for Danny and Helen. Even through her cancer treatments Helen would make time to see me. She was positive and still very funny. We laughed and talked. She was just the strong motherly women who loved a strung out dope fiend just enough, not too much, for me to get up on my feet and become strong enough to love myself.

I was with Danny a few hours before he passed. My grandmother was in the same spot rehabbing to come home also. Danny was fine. Although he was on oxygen he was alert, awake, sitting in his chair in his regular jean shorts, and tee shirt. We spoke of my little girl who had a special place in his heart. He told me I was the real deal. I was his miracle and I was his girl. I said, "Yes Danny I'm your girl and grateful to be here." If I had known this was going to be the last time I would talk to him I would have made plans to go to a steak dinner on my next day off. I told Danny he would have to pay. He said it was a great idea. He died in his sleep a few short hours later.

When I said, "Yes, Danny I'm grateful to be here," it is reference to our Tuesday night Pack Your Shit Meeting. I needed Danny's style of governing. I needed Helen's love. I needed the ABC and the great team of Danny, Helen and Bill W. These people are the strength of my recovery. After we had dinner on Tuesdays, which was always good Mexican food, we would have a PYSM. If you had been passing notes, flirting with the fellows, or breaking the rules you would be told to pack your shit. He would call roll and when he got to your name, you would respond, "Yes Danny I'm grateful to be here, or thank you Danny, yes Danny."

Even my baby would say, "Tank," to Danny. Without these people I would not be the women I am today.

Tim E

I met Danny L on April 10, 1986 when I went to the ABC Club in Indio and asked if I could be admitted there for treatment of my longstanding drug problem. I had recently been arrested for under the influence of a controlled substance and the judge had given me the opportunity to serve my ninety day sentence in a recovery house instead of the county jail, if I could get into one. The court gave me two weeks to try and get in a treatment facility, or I would start my sentence in the county jail. So, on the fourteenth day, I showed up on the doorstep of the ABC Club in Indio and was told by a resident there that I would have to wait around until this guy named Danny L got back if I wanted to try and get admitted. Having really no place else to go I waited there for an hour or so before Danny returned. I went up to him and explained my pitiful situation and asked if he would accept me. Danny looked me straight in the eye and said, "We're full here. We don't have any beds." I started to walk away when I heard him say, "You might be able to find a spot on a couch." I didn't ask any more questions. I had already been given the word by others that if Danny says, "Find a spot on a couch," or "You can hang around," or anything other than, "Get off my property," that I should shut up and take it as tacit acceptance into the ABC Club.

That's exactly what I did. I tried to make myself as inconspicuous as possible because I didn't want to give anybody an excuse to kick me out. Indeed the house was full, very full, but I came to learn that that's how it always was at the ABC Club in Indio. It seemed that this guy Danny L had a real problem turning away an alcoholic, or an addict that was seeking help. I have known Danny now, and his wife for over twenty-three, or more years. That has never changed. Danny's first instinct is always to help the addict, or alcoholic who wants help. Today, in this day and age of recovery as big business, it is astonishing to recall how Danny treated me when I showed up on his doorstep and asked for help. He never even asked me how I intended to pay! Not once. Not ever! He could take one look at me and tell that if I still had a dollar in my pocket I'd be trying to buy a drink, pill, or fix with it. He knew I couldn't pay. That didn't matter to Danny. He just wanted to give me a chance if I was willing to help myself. Money had nothing to do with it.

I didn't really give myself much of a chance to stay clean. I had tried and failed so many times before that I had pretty much given up any hope that I could ever remain drug free. Maybe others could do it, but not me. I knew my case was different. Danny was tough. He didn't put up with any BS from anybody. When it came to recovery Danny was deadly serious. I should take my disease seriously, but I shouldn't take myself too seriously. I've heard him say that a thousand times. Danny always taught that if you can learn to laugh at yourself it was part of the healing process. Addicts and alcoholics need to learn to forgive themselves. Danny L taught me that.

Although I never expected to stay clean, something started working for me during those ninety days at the ABC Club back in 1986. I started going to meetings and working the Twelve Steps, and I went and got a sponsor to help me with the program. I got involved in service and learned that if I was helping the next guy I could get out of myself. That was another lesson learned at the ABC Club in Indio. Although I only stayed there for ninety days. I feel like I never really left. The ABC Club has been my home base for recovery for twenty-three years. That's where I got my first day clean. That's where it all started for me. Eventually I was asked to serve on the board of directors of the ABC Club, which I did for five years. I felt unqualified for that position, but Danny had taught me to suit up, and show up. So that is just what I did. I just looked at it as another way to be of service. I knew I owed a debt of gratitude to the ABC Club that could never be repaid, but if I had a chance to be of service to the ABC Club I should always take advantage of the opportunity.

I have had a front row view of Danny and Helen L working with alcoholics and addicts for over twenty-three years. I have marveled at their work ethic, their persistence and their undying willingness to help those who still suffer from this illness. I have met many people who I admire after being in recovery for twenty-three years, but nobody even comes close to Danny and Helen Leahy. I can only wonder how many 'thousands of lives' these two people have positively impacted through their selfless efforts for over forty years? It's not just the individuals who they have helped to get drug and alcohol free, but all the families of those people and their employers and children, and grandchildren.

A drug addict, or an alcoholic who is in his, or her addiction touches many lives in a very negative way. But a drug addict, or alcoholic who finds recovery can completely turn that around and the ripple effect of their recovery has benefits that radiate out through the generations. The positive impact that Danny and Helen Leahy have had on their community cannot be measured. These are truly my heroes.

Lynne M

In 2003 my house was raided by Riverside County Sheriffs. I was a drug dealer, who was on methamphetamine. Little did I know that this would start my journey with Danny and Helen Leahy and the ABC Club. I wasn't home at the time the house was raided, but my roommate called me to tell me what happened. I was at the casino (my other addiction) and within one hour, the task force came there looking for me. I slipped out the back door with a friend and hid away for the weekend. I turned myself in on a Sunday night to face my consequences. I was arrested and booked into the Indio Jail. I spent the next four days there.

When I was released on my own recognizance, the first thing I went to was the pipe. My court date was one month away in which I planned to get an attorney and get clean and sober. Well I managed to do the first thing and hired a gentleman named Mr. Hurley. He asked me if I was willing to go to rehab, I said, "Yes."

Enter Danny Leahy. I was to meet with Danny the next weekend, at the club, but I couldn't get my act together enough to meet him. Danny left me two messages, and the third message said, "This is Danny Leahy and yyyou dddon't know ttthat I don't call pppeople to ccome here, but yyou nneed to bbe hhere ttoday at 2 o'clock." Oh no, now I was really full of fear. I went and he made me wait in the front office for about an hour. All I saw was a lot of crazy people, and it scared me more. Finally I met the man who was going to help me change my life forever. He was to the point, but I heard some compassion in his voice. He said I needed to be checked in before my court date, and that he thought he could help me. I did not qualify for Prop 36 because of the sales charge, but he said not to worry about that right now.

The day came when I was to check in to the club. I was still using, and couldn't get it together enough to pack my things for rehab. It was getting later in the day and I wanted to run away. My door bell rang, and it was my attorney. He followed me to the ABC Club to make sure I got there. I arrived 'kicking and screaming,' and scared to death. I saw Danny, got my things to my room, and was taken down to dinner. Holy crap, what have I done to myself? All I saw was chaos, and freaky people. I wasn't one of them, was I? I wanted to get to my room as soon as I could.

The next day court was at eight. To my surprise, there was Danny driving the van to take me there. It was August and I was detoxing, and Danny said to me, "I feel for ya kid." He took me to the courtroom and walked in with me. I met my attorney there and Danny sat behind me and never left. I was sentenced to six months in jail, fined and put on probation. The judge then said I could serve my sentence at the ABC Club. I didn't know at that time that Danny's presence in the courtroom allowed me to serve my time at the club. I was grateful. Danny put up with my crying and need to run, but kept telling me to surrender. He put me to work in the kitchen. The ABC Club became my home for the next six months, and I swear I felt God's presence there.

Danny and Helen helped me so much without judgment. About two months after I was there I asked Bill W, who was the financial officer, how I was going to pay for my time there. Could I make payments? He said that it was taken care of. I will never know how or why, but I never had to pay for my time there. Danny and Helen and the staff, should never be forgotten for the thousands of people they helped and the many lives they saved through their hard work and the message of recovery. I will always be grateful to them, and will never forget what they did for me. I never went back to using meth.

Dani M

Coming to Indio, California was not my first choice, but it was my last chance for freedom and I did not want to be locked up again. So, here I was in my battered 'ole Monza hatchback (yes I said Monza) it had a big hole in the floor board and plenty of dents to identify it for what it was - an addict's home. It contained most of what was left of my life's possessions and me - or at least what was left of me; broken in ways we are not supposed to be broken. And I brought what I thought was a big secret with me.

This was not my first rodeo in a treatment center. I had been in three other centers over the past five years, but I simply could not believe in anything enough to give recovery a real chance. My big secret was, I was scheduled in Banning Court on the day I arrived at ABC Recovery Center, where I was supposed to be locked up for two years and eight months for a list of felonies I committed trying to protect my right to use speed, weed, and alcohol. Also, I had not been successful at the court mandated treatment centers and the court was ready to stop my nonsense. I did not tell any of that to the lady who took my calls and finally told me there was a couch for me to sleep on if I could get to Indio.

I don't know when I became so desperate to stop living the way I was living. I just knew I was finally all out of good ideas. I saw it as God stepping in front of one more bullet for me and I knew I would mess it up, but I would try to be good for as long as I could. I did not know anything about addiction, or alcoholism, so just thought I must be a bad person. At the time I thought I might get to stay clean for a little while until the obsession to use got to be too strong. They kept me very busy at ABC, especially the first few weeks! I attended two to three AA or NA meetings a day along with daily chores, groups, finding and using a sponsor, step-work and structured social activities. Susan Van Winkle was assigned to be my advocate and I was directed to talk to her, or to the director of women, Helen Leahy, whenever I had a concern, or question about what action I should take next. I was firmly directed to NOT discuss my needs, or ideas with the male staff, or residents.

I needed to learn healthy relationship skills and that was not going to happen if I continued to act in old behavior.

Danny Leahy and Bill W became my first healthy male role models in sobriety. Between them, they appeared in court with me in Banning almost every month for as long as I lived at the club. We (one of them, another woman from the house, and myself) would leave Indio by six-thirty a.m. and typically not return until after six p.m. due to the fact that I was always the last person to be seen by the judge. The drive to Banning was always filled with dread and negative thoughts for me because I knew the damage I had caused, and I knew the judge could put me into custody at any time. Neither Danny, nor Bill seemed all too concerned and each time I was released into their custody I was relieved and grateful. Our drives home were marked with their comments of what a mess I had caused and stories of the antics they had experienced while drinking. I started to wonder if maybe I wasn't a bad person. The seed was planted that alcoholism is a disease and I just might have it.

I lived at the Doll House for two months and became very close to Susan Van Winkle due to our long late night talks when I was unable to sleep. She was tireless when it came to walking me through some difficulty I was unable to resolve. I connected with her southern upbringing and down home, straight from the heart talks. She truly cared for me and encouraged me to begin to feel loved.

As time passed and my job became full time I was moved to the transition house across the alley. Bea (housemother) became my advocate and I learned to take 'baby steps' instead of trying so hard to do everything in a single bound. I began to see the value in living one day at a time from watching Bea. I learned to live with other women and to find joy in being still with God. I was reunited with my family and I began to grow in the AA community because of the lessons I learned in that house.

Helen taught me to be discerning when it came to trusting others. She made it clear that not everyone could, or should be trusted. She asked me regularly to seek my Higher Power for answers and not so much to seek what other people thought. Danny quizzed me on the Twelve Traditions on a regular basis, often asking, "What Tradition covers that?" when I would announce some plan I had. The most common answer was Tradition Four which includes the phrase, 'Don't take yourself too damn seriously.' Bill would remind me that doing the same thing and expecting different results was insanity and I should maybe try a different action.

I lived under the ABC umbrella for a little more than nineteen months and in that time I was gifted with so many things. I found knowledge of the disease of alcoholism and the program of recovery that equips me with the tools I need to live free of any mood, or mind altering chemical. I was granted peace and strength in my Higher Power. I discovered that making and keeping commitments is a blessing that allows me to reflect the love I have found. I learned that loved ones die, and others move on, and even in the pain of those losses someone is standing right beside me ready to take my hand and help me find comfort. And the most precious gift I received is the gift of personal freedom that comes from learning to love and to be loved, unconditionally. DOS 10/25/1995

Duane H

I came to the club for recovery. I didn't want to go there. The judge, in Utah, had received a letter from the ABC Club saying I could go there. The judge said I got off on two felonies, in Utah, and he hoped if I went to the club I'd get recovery. So I had to go from there.

I was scared. I didn't know anyone, in a town I'd never been in before. At first I was in the Pack Your Shit Meeting. I was trying to talk to the guy next to me. He got pissed off and told me to shut up. I had no idea why he told me to shut up. Then I found out that that was the PYSM and that if you got in trouble you were kicked out. The guy next to me didn't want to get kicked out.

I was unsure about Danny and Helen. Danny was a little scary and seemed everybody was scared of him. Calling people assholes and kicking them out of the program at the PYSM. I was there for fifteen months.

When I left I felt I had learned a lot, had a good program, a good foundation, and had money, because of their savings plan. I had money enough to get my own place at sober living, had a job, and was saving money to be out on my own.

There was the time that the club had a program to help people with teeth. Danny, Bill and Mario took me to Mexico to get some teeth. I had one tooth and it was on a flipper so I got to get real teeth. I hadn't smiled in years because I had one front tooth caused from my life on drugs. It boosted my moral. It was real nice to be able to smile again and kind of let loose with my dentures made in Mexico. I felt better about myself. I could smile and be happy instead of being serious, and not able to smile.

I come to find out Danny really did love us. With his facade of being mean and calling us assholes I finally figured out if he was too nice to us we wouldn't straighten out our shit. I went to CODA (Co-dependents Anonymous) with Helen. Helen was a real loving caring lady. I ended up loving them both and I'm proud to be an alumnus of ABC Recovery Center. ABC helped save my life, and other peoples lives. Saved my families lives, saved my mom. Saved my ex-wife's life. Saved my only daughter's life.

Pat D

I arrived at the ABC Recovery Center because I needed to learn a different way to live. I am an alcoholic. I was so out of control, that I had lost everyone and everything that that was important in my life. I finally figured that the world would be better off without me, so I attempted suicide. I could not even get that right, and finally ended up in recovery for the first, and hopefully the only time.

I had spent some time at the club before, but not as a resident. I was attending one meeting during the week, but then I would leave and go right back to old behavior. Clearly I should not have been allowed to leave, so when I did arrive as a resident, it sort of felt like I was at home.

Danny and Helen scared me at first, but the more time I spent there, the more I enjoyed their company. Danny was extremely devoted to the residents. The stories he told about his own journey of recovery were very inspiring, and I always enjoyed the nightly walk. I remember a saying of his to this day; "If the palm trees are moving then it's not that hot."

I was an actual resident for about six months, then I moved to a sober living house for another six, or seven months. It was nice to be able to transition out of the club before being thrown back into the world. The best things were making new friends, attending meetings and classes all day, and the endless pot of coffee. The worst part of being at the club was seeing good friends leave, and go back to suffering with addiction.

So now, I have seventeen plus years sober and clean. I have been extremely blessed to have my children back in my life, and now I have eight beautiful grandchildren, I have become a much better grandma than I was a mom, because of staying sober and clean. I have my first college degree, and I have been in a committed relationship for over sixteen years. I never realized that my life could be so complete. Thanks Danny and Helen, and all the staff who were present at the ABC Recovery Center at the time I was there.

Paula S (Daughter of a resident).

My memories of the ABC Club are some of the best of my life! I remember being absolutely thrilled when the weekend would come, and my dad would drive me to Indio. Everyone there were like the awesome family I never had. I remember one night Danny taking me to Naugles for a bean and cheese burrito, and then to Gemco to buy me a sweatshirt. Remember Gemco? And remember when we would go to Bob's Big Boy after the Friday night meeting for coffee and dessert. Just thinking about it makes me want to cry. Those were some of the best times of my life!

I remember the night I met Brandon, and he and I took a walk over to a gal's place (Sherry whose mom was in the program). He joked with me that it was like a five mile hike. He really got a kick out of messing with me. Remember Laura, the house mother? I just adored her. When she would go away for the weekends I got to sleep in her bed in the girl's house, which I loved. I remember the night Heidi got there too. She looked like she just rolled out from underneath a tumbleweed. (Heidi came from the hobo's camp by the railroad. It took 3 baths to get her clean). I really do need to write my next play about the club. There are just too many great stories from that place. In fact - I had my very first kiss on the steps behind the club (a horrible kiss, I might add, but my first kiss nonetheless).

Paula S (same daughter of a resident, now an adult)

My first residential stay at the ABC Recovery Center (formerly known as the ABC Club) occurred in June of 2005. I'd like to share with you how a moment of clarity ushered me through those double doors, but that just wasn't the case. In actuality, methamphetamine psychosis drove me to seek refuge at the place I'd called a second home since I was ten. My mother, Kay, had been first a resident and then an employee. For Christ's sake, I had my first kiss on the steps behind what's now the men's detox house when I was fourteen.

But in June of 2005 when I packed up and drove myself to Indio - I was an emaciated, gut-sick, paranoid shell of what I'd been as a teenager. Not so much interested in recovery as I was a welcoming home, a familiar face, a little love, and this place was the closest to all of that for me; four walls that held some of the fondest memories of my youth. And although I was secretly angry at Danny for refusing to hold a memorial service for my mother when she died in 1999, I was more relieved than pissed to be in he and Helen's presence once more. My mother, after all, kinda fucked them over.

But about a month into my stay, my brains still fried from months of meth use. I got distracted. I fucked up. But not with meth. With men, my other addiction. Well in this case, a boy. One obsession morphed into another when I began a secret affair with a nineteen-year-old male resident whose endearing advances I could hardly resist. And, he was fine! And, he could ride a skateboard like nobody's business, a fetish of mine. Before I'd begun my first step, Mike and I were sneaking away on weekends to fraternize at my white stucco house in Desert Hot Springs. Not a wise way to be carrying on when you're living under Danny Leahy's roof! Anyone who knew Danny has undoubtedly heard the phrase 'Pack your shit' uttered innumerable times on any given Tuesday in the ABC dining hall. If ever there was a day of the week during the summer of 2005 when all my paranoia came rushing back, it was as I sat there certain Danny was about to call me out, as the a..a..a..a..sshole I knew I was, during his infamous Pack Your Shit Meetings.

But miraculously, it never happened. Mike and I got away with our affair while still residents, but went on to practically kill each other in the dark months that followed completion of the sixty day program. And although our tumultuous, drug-fueled affair has long since expired, the boy and I remain friends. And by the grace of God, I haven't snorted a line of speed in more than six years, but that would take a second visit to ABC.

Steve S

I showed up at the ABC Club August 1st 1990. My probation officer told me to go to Indio, to the ABC Club and get some free tools. I thought 'Oh boy get some free tools, get back to work, get some money, and I'd be on my way.' That's when I found out the free tools were from AA (patience, tolerance, honesty etc.). Seeing as I had no place else to go I stuck around. Bill W welcomed me. Took me under his wing, and told me to stay here and behave. Don't go to jail. Do what is suggested, like it, or not. The next day I got hustled off to Madd Dog Daze (a local August convention), to be a greeter. Not feeling one hundred percent at all, and I was scared to death, but it worked out. Things had a way of working out. That was my first encounter of things I didn't understand working out. The ABC Club, Madd Dog Daze, or any of that.

I'd already gone to AA for two DUIs, before going to the ABC Club, but I just wasn't ready. This time I guess I was ready, because it just seemed to work. I didn't hear anything in AA the first time around. I was at the ABC Club eleven months. I was glad to get out of there. By then I was ready to be out of there. I knew what to do and what not to do and I haven't had any trouble since. I was pretty comfortable. Sometimes my mouth gets me in trouble, but I haven't got into any trouble drinking. No drinking trouble.

Nicole T

Danny and Helen saved my life. I was twenty years old. I'm diabetic and I came out of a coma involving drugs and alcohol. I went into the ABC Club. I didn't quite understand what it was about, only because I was not ready. When Danny called me an asshole I didn't know that meant he loved me. I took it the other way instead of him loving me.

Helen would have those women's groups where we would talk about healthy relationships versus the non-healthy. I remember being in an unhealthy relationship. I remembered what she had taught me and I left that relationship.

Danny and Helen were always loving and caring. Where I work now, it's really important to me to be part of somewhere where it's a helping community and helping people. That's what they did. There was no turn a ways. I was on the couch numerous times. They were full, but they allowed me to be on the couch. It was always my home away from home for sure.

I've got all phone numbers, even my parents, numerous friends and I've never forgot the ABC Club number, or address. I'm now a lead counselor at Russ Intensive Outpatient. I go to church. I'm going into a program that is being established where I start going into the jails and institutions to do counceling. It's being created by a group of people, and what it is, is to bring it back to the old AA. It should be interesting.

I finally got tired of being sick and tired. Everything they ever told me, I find myself telling my clients the same thing. The things that were shared with me that I needed to do for my recovery are the same things I tell my own clients. I go to meetings and I sponsor women. Part of the fourth step work has been lost. There's a book called <u>Carry the Message by Joe Peal.</u> It's about the old AA and bringing back the traditions. And that part of the step work has been lost.

I went to the club twice on Prop. 36. The last time with the new people. I do believe I learned so much from both times. I swear that I wouldn't be in the position I'm in if it hadn't been for David L. I lived with him for a while. I'm sorry that people separated. The old clan and the new clan. I got to experience both worlds. I did my internship there.

They both served a purpose for me. I look back to six years ago, and where I was then to where I am today, and it just blows my mind. The reason I'm where I'm at today is because I follow directions. I completely turn it over and follow directions.

Dixie S

In 1991 my sister came to Las Vegas to pick me up and take me to Indio, California. She knew I needed help so she took me to the ABC Club. I had no idea what I was walking into. We were late for the Sunday Night Candle Light Meeting, so she took me through the back door. It was a big room and flickering lights throughout. A women was sharing from the podium and a candle shadowed her face. She talked about real feelings and things women alcoholics' do to support their alcoholism and addictions. Then she talked about how her life is different today. I was so attracted to our program instantly.

The next morning I met Danny and Helen. I was scared of them at first. The very most important thing I can say about them is that they loved alcoholics. They understood us much better then we understood ourselves. Every time they spoke my life changed. I am so grateful for the ABC Club which was Danny and Helen.

I lived there for one and a half years and slowly got my life together. By learning how to be responsible for my recovery and in AA I learned how to be responsible for myself and my life. The day before I left I was in the PYSM and Danny said I was catatonic, and my first thought was...what does that mean? Later I learned what it meant, and he was right. I was so proud and honored that he would say that to me. It still makes me happy.

Sue B

The Loss is the Gift/The Gift is the Loss

I was asked several months ago (too many to admit) to write something about Danny and Helen. My first response was, "Of course." After several months of procrastination I begin to tackle the job. Why the delay? I have only this answer. Too much to say, too many emotions, not enough pages to express, and of course the feelings of loss now that they are both gone. While some may say that it is not a loss as we were blessed to know them and were blessed by their being and gifts they gave so many of us. I have since suffered another great loss in the past year hence it was too much for me to face at first.

As I sit here now though, almost one whole year since Danny's been gone, and reflect I can identify and cherish the gifts both he and Helen gave me and countless others. As those of us, ABCer's from back in the day, continue our path and journey in recovery, we do what they taught us which is to show up, no matter what, share our experience, strength and hope with others and be of service to those in need. Many faces come and go, so many people, so many treatment centers, so many different twists to the steps, the program and how it works. So much darkness searching for light. We reflect at how fortunate we were.. those of us who were blessed to hit our bottoms and crawl into, or get dropped off in Indio, California at the ABC Club when Danny and Helen were running the show.

My first personal memories were terror, laughter, men, women, babies, trains, food, routine, loneliness, togetherness, differences, commonalities, groups, learning and crying. I was alone, afraid, and desperate. This just covers the internal part. Externally there were losses, both legal and custody issues ahead that I was not even yet able to understand. I was in a haze of unknown and uncharted territory. Helen scared me and I was not even sure what to make of Danny. All I knew was that my existence was in their hands... or so I was told.

I was soon exposed to groups, meetings, books, steps, counseling and mutual compassion from both residents and staff members. There were so many powerful influences that I can lump together. So many people who impacted those early days. Danny and Helen yes, but the package included: Bill, Sunny, Mary, Kenny, Roger, Tony, Susan, Debbie, Mario, Dino, Gay Henchy, Donna, Pam, Debbie S, Charlie, Patrick, Gary, Lorraine, Alice, Berta, Sharon... the list goes on. I am so fortunate to have been introduced to all these amazing people who shared their experiences and words with me in one-way or another. So many conversations, so many tears, so much laughter. Life changing times that came from hitting an unconceivable bottom that no one previously could have helped me, or guided me through.

While it is true that the above people played a huge role in the early days of shaping and changing my life, the real juice came from the dynamic combination of Danny and Helen. Helen was, as I stated, scary at first, however once I allowed myself to hear her and her ideas, thoughts and experiences, my life would be changed and shaped into the sober women I am today. She identified patterns and losses in my life that added to my inabilities in life, enhancing, not causing my disease, all while affecting each of my relationships. And Danny too much to say, but if I had to sum it up I would have to say he taught me to not be a victim, to take responsibility for my actions, to own up to my behavior, and flat out that if I don't want to feel a certain way, don't do the action that will cause it. They both gave me the gift of loving me enough to not worry about hurting my feelings.

While it may sound simple, what each of them gave to so many others and me, it was not. People like me over complicate matters, think too hard, and have pushed away any form of advice, or assistance for years upon years. So it was their delivery, understanding and disposition that changed so many of us. So is it a loss, if we gained so much? Knowing them, being in their 'club' during those times was truly a gift. The gift is that I learned about myself, repaired relationships, and began my life; the loss is not having them here with us anymore. The gift, that they touched so many of us that we now hold each other up without knowing it, the loss is that they are not here with us anymore. The gift, that they taught us how to have a better life and to help others who are in need find their way; the loss is that they are not here with us anymore. So what is the loss, if they gave us such a gift? As we all continue to give what they taught us, there is no loss. If the loss is that they are not here with us anymore, yet we are all continuing their message onto others, than aren't they in fact here with us after all?

Joann M

The first time I got to the club was in '91. I didn't have a place to live and I asked them if I could stay there. I stayed there for three months. I did everything they asked me to do and thought I would be alright, I stayed sober until '93, but ended up relapsing. I stayed out there until August 13, 1994.

I went into detox in '94. Danny and Helen were on vacation. They always went on vacation in August. I'd been relapsing on drugs and I couldn't do it anymore. My body wasn't functioning the way I thought it should be functioning. I was asking for help one more time. They put me in detox for seven days. I stayed there for seven days and then ended up in another recovery center in Victorville, and I stayed there for three months. While I was there I was communicating with Danny and Helen because I was trying to get back to the program in this end of the valley. They allowed me to come back. To the meetings, outpatient, and the groups. CPS (Child Protective Services) had got involved this time and had taken my child away, My son, because I was out in Victorville, had tried to commit suicide while I was in the other recovery center.

I reached out to Danny and let him know what was going on. Danny was really upset about the whole situation and took me under his wing, Helen too. But I was more connected to Danny because he helped my son to look at life a different way. Danny had gone through some similar situations when he was young. He took my son under his wing and mentored him. He would take him places; like a baseball game. He encouraged my son and told him he was going to be okay. He helped me look at life differently. That life was better without drugs and alcohol. That was my addiction, I liked everything. He helped me to understand a different way to live.

I continued going to meetings. I asked Danny, "How long do I have to go to meetings?"

Danny said, "'Till you want it. For the rest of your life probably."

Now I have going on twenty years clean. I was working and doing what I'm supposed to be doing in recovery. In '96 I lost my job and I didn't have no place to go. I still stayed focused and going to meetings and I would talk to Danny and Helen all the time. I asked them if I could stay at one of the sober living houses. They allowed me to stay, and with my son, even though he was not of the age for sober living. He was about thirteen-years old. At first we stayed at Sirocco House until HUD closed it down. So they ended up letting me stay at the McGovern House. We were there about nine months until I got on my feet. I started working and paying rent there. I had five years when I went into sober living, and I started looking at the structure of life differently. I was feeling more comfortable. But while we were there my son ended up going in and out of Charter. Danny assured me he would be alright and he would take me to visit.

They never looked at me as if they were better than me. They always tried to help a lot of men, and women. I had a good relationship with Helen. I used to go help her clean her house. We used to have lunches and private conversations. I learned how to be intimate with another person. I thought the word intimate meant you have to have sex with anybody. I learned how to be intimate just having a conversation with a person. Be close to people and put your guard down.

When I got there I got there really tore up. I was so dysfunctional that I didn't trust anybody. When I was out there using all the people that were around me hurt me emotionally, mentally, physically. At the ABC Club it was more peer oriented. People were connected. We got to learn personalities. I really loved going to the meetings and events, and when they had the alumni gatherings.

I've always had a relationship with Danny and Helen. I looked up to Danny like he was a father figure, and a grandpa to my son. Helen I looked to as a friend. I always wanted to be like her. Real spiritual and open. Today how I live my life, my work, I'm nice, and I'm not that angry person anymore. My life is so full now. When Helen got sick and she passed on part of me went with her. I was really connected to her. A person I would never forget and I will always treasure her friendship. She would tell you how it was. She never lied to you and didn't sugarcoat anything. Even though she might hurt your feelings. She wasn't doing it to be mean. She told us to be willing to do anything, and anything was possible.

Today I'm spiritual. Open to anything. Willing to learn different things. I don't take my life too serious. I do a lot of meetings. I still go to the ABC Recovery Center and support other people because when I got there they welcomed me. They nurtured me. I love myself and the women I am today.

Danny when he called me an asshole. I asked him one day, "Why do you call people assholes if you don't even know them?"

He said, "That's my way of showing them I love them. If I don't pay attention to you it means I see right through you." He saw right through me because I was a little asshole. The first thing he called me was 'the barracuda.' That I was after the men. That was part of my addiction too. Today I'm not like that. I'm in a relationship today with a man and I can say he's a man. He treats me like a women. I don't let anyone treat me less or belittle me. I got self respect through the program. I'm not that little girl that was afraid of everything and didn't trust anybody. Today I do trust, and give people the benefit of doubt.

Danny and Helen gave me courage and hope; a lot of hope. It wasn't just the program of AA or NA that helped me understand a new way of life. We had a lot of fun and laughed a lot with them. They never steered me wrong. I never put them up on a pedestal because they were just human beings like me.

I haven't had the desire to drink, or use. I continue going to meetings; three meetings a week and I help a lot of women. I sponsor a lot of women. Helen was my grand sponsor. Even when she was sick with cancer she looked at life very positive. She was not a negative person. She didn't believe she was going to die. She still worked at Leather Plus. She did not ever feel sorry for herself. I did when I got here. I want to be like her. Danny and Helen gave me my life back. I was so lost I never thought I'd be doing some of the things I have. Go on trips, vacations, I've gone on cruises. I've done lots of things because I look at life positive. They didn't turn their backs on me.

My son still struggles through life but he never forgets Danny and Helen. I don't know how I could ever repay them. When he was fourteen years old he wanted to go do this boxing thing in Coachella and Danny bought all the stuff for him. Every year he would buy my son's school clothes, backpack and paper and pencils and didn't ask for anything in return.

Danny said, "Joann, all I want you to do is keep doing this deal on a daily basis. Don't use no matter what." And that is my payback to him. I do it because I love the way my life is today. When I look back my life was really horrible. Today I have hope, courage, and faith. I have the God of my understanding. As long as I keep going to meetings and doing the things I do today I'll be happy.

Robin B

I got to the ABC Club in June of 2001 for my first round. I had tried a detox before then, but that was the time when I got in and stayed for six months. When I first got there I couldn't even comb my hair. I was on a severe detox watch and I had a hat put on my head. When I first went in they were having the AID's project. The AID's people came in and they did the film and were talking about HEP-C. It really touched me because I knew a women in Texas who had it. I remember being in the dining hall. The new house hadn't been built yet and everything happened in the cafeteria, the main room. The offices were there and you couldn't really get away with anything.

The other thing that was dreadful and exciting at the same time was the PYSM. My voice would always be after the girl with the squeaky voice that said, "Yes I want to be here."

And then I said with my deep voice, "Yes I want to be here."

Danny asked me, because of the six months run, "Are you going to stay here asshole, or are you going to run?" It was up to Danny's discretion whether, or not I could stay.

I loved the Tuesday night book study of <u>Women Who Love too Much.</u> That was the group Helen ran, and we got in there and talked about everything. It was a scramble learning to live life and all those different personalities. It really was a gift that I got from them. It was the gift of sobriety. I did learn to put things back where they belong. And the sweeps, were they would shut down the kitchen.

On that first run on two separate occasions when they had the Sunday morning meeting I heard my story come out of a man's mouth. I was dumbfounded. 'I thought really?' Also Albertine Roed was taking her cake. We were all in that enclosed room and we were very tight. I was thinking my God if this women can do it, I can do it. But I did go back out.

I relapsed. Danny would get up there and stand at the podium and say, "God shook me, and woke me up, and said I got to come down here and put a curse on you." I realized that once you get recovery under your belt for any increment of time, and you go out, it isn't easy because you got a head full of knowledge knowing there is another way of life, and a belly full of booze.

Then when I relapsed I came back in August '02. Lucky Debbie and Mary where there and I was pregnant with my son. I was very grateful that ABC had the women's program. I could only put together a week at a time and knew I had to get back under Mary's discretion, and I went and talked to Mary. She said only under the condition, and she'd have to talk to Danny, to see if they'd let me in, but I'd have to be on restriction until I had the baby.

That was it. I was to go nowhere without someone with me. Being pregnant at ABC was definitely different then the other time; because I was down on the bottom floor with all the girls.

Danny took me to get my son's first outfit. He was running around and I wasn't allowed to leave the property. But I had finally got some money and he let me ride with him and I got to go in Target and pick out the baby's first outfit.

I remember the pictures with Danny, and the dances and ABC got a comedy show that they contracted with Mark L and that was fabulous. One of the most memorable things was Danny saying, "What are you going to do?" Danny also helped me get a car. The ABC at that time had the baby birthday awards and I was going to get mine. I was in a pinch and I wasn't due to have mine yet. I went and talked to Danny and he said, "What? No. Are you crazy? Explain it to me again." It was like no I'm not giving you the damn money. Then I went and talked to Mary and she said Danny okayed it.

The ABC gave me a new life so I could have a successful life and I wouldn't have been able to get a car if it hadn't been for him saying it was okay.

I was struggling a lot with guilt from the past. I was at a crossroads. Do I stay sober, or do I say 'screw it' and go get loaded again. Do I use guilt as an excuse. I went in to talk to Helen in her office. She was sitting behind her desk as she did. I was troubled and I explained it to her. She was very calm and she did that thing were she processed it. She said, "You know Robin, nothing in God's world happens by mistake," and she chewed her gum. It was just like she had the right answer and I knew it. Danny and Helen were both God's earth angels, and they touched so many lives. Just watching how they were so good with one girl who had alcohol/drug psychosis.

One girl couldn't stand my snoring and she was bitching, and bitching, and moaning and wanted me out. They did move me to another room.

One day I was in the office all concerned with my mail and staff was all in there. Mail slots hung on the wall behind the door. Some times I can be nosy, but I could hear everything that was going on there. Danny looks at me. They were having some kind of an important conversation. He said, "Can you get out of here? God dang it." He was scary, but it was a good thing. He also would say, "We'll give you enough rope to hang your self."

He would always say, "It's none of my business what you think of me, what I think about me is what counts."

I was there for a year. I lived in the Doll House for six months. I had my baby, who was born healthy because of ABC on November of '02. I got to do the Christmas party and then I stayed for another two months there. Then I got to go to the McGovern House for six months until things came together and I was able to move out on my own. I continued to do the ABC Aftercare Program, and do meetings, and I stayed connected to the people there. It will always be my home.

I went to College of the Desert after that. I remember going and talking to Helen. One of the first classes Helen helped me because I did a paper on the birth of AA. She gave me the resources for the paper. I've been clean and sober eleven years. My son is eleven-years too. I'm older than him. I did get my associates degree. I'm currently working forty hours a week and looking forward to new horizons.

Jessie G

I went though the ABC Club. The first time I got there was 1994. I was introduced to this gentleman by the name of Danny Leahy and his wife Helen. I went in there with the intentions of somewhat staying clean and sober. They told me the truth about myself. They said I wasn't ready. That I was trying to be hip, slick and cool. That is one of the best things that I loved about Danny and Helen. They were always straight and forward with me. They always told me the truth. At that time I thought they didn't care, or that they didn't like me. Being a Mexican was one of those things. So I went back out.

He was right because I came back in the ABC Club in 1998. He greeted me with charming words. "How you doing asshole? Was it any different for you out there?"

Of course I told him, "No."

He says, "Are you still hip, slick and cool?"

I said, "Well, I don't think so. I have no where to go. I'm at the bitter end of my road and I need help."

Here is another thing about those loving people that I truly respect, and a big part of my recovery today was that when I went in there they never charged me a penny. And that when they ran the house, the ABC Club, it was so recovery orientated. It was always about recovery. They truly expressed meetings, sponsorship, and the Twelve Steps of the fellowship. One of the greatest things the ABC Club and these lovely people did was introduce me to my fellowship.

I was there nine months. I stayed clean ever since and am coming up on sixteen years. Danny and Helen were both great friends of mine. Nobody ever trusted me, and Danny told me, "Jessie I'm trusting you with my car. That's the difference today. When you first came in I wouldn't let you near my car. Today you can fix my car."

Today I'm clean. I've been a productive, responsible member of society. I owe these people so much. Danny said, "It's one hand helping another." I've been doing that ever since. As a result of that I've maintained clean and sober in the world. My life today is just great as a result of working the Twelve Steps as he spoon fed me. He engraved that into me and I've maintained the spiritual principals.

I just love the ABC Club. That is my house. I protect that house. Even today. I wish Danny and Helen was still here. One day I was slouching down on the couch. He said, "Sit your ass up." I thought that was kind of cruel, but that's the way I needed to be talked to at that time. If they had talked to me any nicer I probably wouldn't be here today. I'm truly grateful that I met those people, and went through the ABC Club facility, and that God put them in my life. I'm glad he made this recovery house what it was while he was there. It flourished. He and Helen helped so many people. Today I give back.

Marjorie H

I came to the ABC Recovery Center in July of 1991 because I was pregnant. Not because I felt like I had a drinking and using issue. I came so I could have a clean baby. Two of the factors that helped me get there were; my brother had been to ABC a few times and he was always talking about it, and a friend of mine and me were hanging out on a corner, and she saw her kids in a car with their foster parents. She had lost custody of them. We saw them come to the corner in our neighborhood, where we were hanging out, and buy crack. I didn't want that to happen to me so I came to ABC.

I enjoyed the experience. I tried to learn all I could in any meetings that I had to attend. And to this day I still kind of know the schedule. I tried to get something out of it. I was there so I made the most of it. I stayed there a year because that's what they recommended. The Doll House was my son's first home. It was a real nice place to live. The staff and counselors were there to help you get your life together.

Danny and Helen were loved and respected and they wanted us to get our lives together. It wasn't about what we could give them for Christmas. They wanted us to get our lives together and they did what they could to make that happen. What I really liked about Danny and Helen was that they were down to earth. You'd see them hanging out playing cards or dominos with the residents. Just kicking it like regular folks. I'll always love and respect them for what they started and kept going and how they wanted to help the addict and alcoholic.

So the first time I got there I stayed clean and sober for two and a half years. I went back out after that. When I left ABC after a year I moved back in with my biggest resentment, which is my mom. I wasn't aware of it at the time, but that is where my son and I moved to. I ended up going back out. The reason I ended up going back out is because I did not work a program. I didn't hardly go to any meetings. I didn't work with my sponsor. I had gone through my steps with her, but after I left I didn't maintain a program.

The second time I came to ABC was July of '96. I've been clean and sober ever since that time; for seventeen and a half years. It's a miracle that I haven't drank and used for the seventeen and a half years. What I consider is my miracle of stopping smoking cigarettes. When I was five years clean and sober I prayed one time to ask God to take the cigarettes too. He took them and it's like I never smoked.

What I learned the second time was that you have to surrender to win. The first time I came because I was pregnant. I didn't think I had a drug problem. I didn't get high every day. Maybe two, three days out of the week I'd get high. The second time I came back I was getting high every day. I might have missed a day here and there. Just before I became a resident again at ABC I was coming to meetings, and I came to the Relapse Prevention Meeting one afternoon. In that meeting they talked about surrender and I learned there that I had to surrender to win. That's what I knew I had to do and I accepted it. By the time they called and said they had a bed I had two weeks clean and sober. I didn't have to stand up as a newcomer for thirty days. I liked that.

Now days what I do is go to meetings. In order to have a program you've got to maintain it, you got to go to meetings, you've got to give back. You have to work a program. Family will say, "You still got to go to those meetings?"

I tell them, "Yeah, I still go to them, and you could use a meeting."

Danny and Helen were very active and helping the residents. They participated, led groups, and meetings. They didn't put it off on other staff members. They were totally involved in the daily operation of ABC Recovery Center. I loved that it was a mom and pop operation. Danny and Helen were both down to earth. Danny was especially down to earth. What I really loved and respected about Helen is how in our Candlelight Meetings on Thursday nights, the women would share, and after while Helen would share, and give us some guidance, direction, and share her wisdom with us. Sunny would do it too, and Trish. I love these women and I'll always love and respect them. They kind of helped me get back on track.

I'm not going to give total credit to ABC, but they did play a big part in my recovery. What I tell my Pastor is that I need the process of the Twelve Steps, but God is the bottom line. When I first got to ABC and we got to Step Three I thought, hummm, it sounds like they are trying to trick you into believing in God. But I would listen and I heard a lady at a NA convention say that NA helped her find God. In my case the

Twelve Step recovery program, and the ABC Recovery Center, and me being involved helped me modify my approach to the same God I grew up with. As far as I'm concerned there is only one God.

So I consider myself working a faith based Christian recovery. If I understand this correctly all of this came out of the Bible. If you research back far enough it all came out of the Bible. For each step there is some scripture to go along with it. When I'm sitting in meetings I'll notice stuff and, oh, we do that in church all the time. There's similarities. I always include God in my prayers. In NA in the Third Step Prayer they want to leave God out. I want God to take my will and my life and guide me in my recovery and show me how to live. I don't want to just say take my will and life. I want God in it.

The son that I had in the ABC Recovery Center is twenty-two now. He needs to go to some meetings himself. I can't make him do anything

I remember Christmas time. I grew up in a family of six children and I'm the oldest girl. That meant I had to be a parent, or mom's helper. I'm always looking out for the younger ones; my siblings under me. I have a brother who is older. At Christmas time we got four, five gifts with the house. Then the women used to have their own party. We could eat. The ladies that didn't live there would bring food. They would bring us gifts. I got a lot of gifts for Christmas. I enjoyed that because I had never got so much. We didn't have a lot growing up. My Mom worked hard and when she could she bought us nice quality stuff. Not cheap stuff.

I'm not like a lot of people. They didn't finish high school. They didn't really do anything productive before they got to recovery. I was thirty-nine-years old the first time I came. I had finished high school. I had gone to college, and got my AA. I had gone on to San Diego State. Then I ended up dropping out because I was tired of school. After five years of going to college I got to take a break.

This time around I ended up going back to college. I had been out of school thirty-five years. I got my substance abuse certificate. By the time I finished it my son had me stressed out and I wasn't trying to counsel anybody.

I appreciate the experience at ABC. I can never thank Danny and Helen enough. They were always hospitable. Just before Danny passed he said, "Come over anytime." I'll always be grateful for the ABC Center. They helped me get my life back on track. I need ABC and I need church as well because God is the bottom line.

My son and I consider the ABC Recovery Center our second home. People who get to go there and be residents, and everybody doesn't get the chance for the merry go round of life to stop, let you off, and acquire some skills to help you go forward in life. I'll forever be grateful for ABC and for Danny and Helen, Bill and Sunny, Mary and Ken, and the staff, and residents of ABC Recovery Center. I'll always feel fortunate and blessed to have been a resident there two times.

Laurie P

I came down here in 1991 after numerous other rehabs. My family found out about it through a friend of a friend. They thought I might be able to do better in Indio than I had at the other ones. They dropped me off and were going to Africa. Picture them out in the bush in Kenya eating with Maasai Mora warriors standing next to them to keep the animals at bay. They ate at big tables with silver domes over their food. Then went and stayed for five nights in Paris in the hotel that overlooks the American Embassy. And I'm at the ABC Club in Indio. They had a ticket for me to go first class all the way to Africa. I drank it up and ended up in Indio.

I came down totally unwilling. I lasted about one month and one week. The first weekend I went out, I went out.

I had met people at the club and sixteen months later I called KK to see if she would talk to Danny. Danny said there's no way that I could get back in. A few days later she called me to say that Danny had gone on vacation and Bill would let me in if I got there that day. So I quickly came down and Bill told me, "Make sure you're doing everything you should be doing because if you're not Danny will kick you out when he comes back." Apparently I was doing everything I was supposed to because I didn't get kicked out.

Danny looked at me and just glared and said, "What are you doing here?" and walked away and that was that. I went running and crying to Bill.

Bill said, "Don't worry he will be okay. He's not going to kick you out as long as you are doing the right thing." I didn't get kicked out. I stayed there for 110 days. Had no thought that I would be able to stay sober because it had been so hard to in the past. Really didn't think anything was different.

One morning I was on the van going from the club to Fellowship Hall. I looked at the Hyatt Hotel on Hwy 111 and all of a sudden the flowers were out and the grass was really green. I thought that was a spiritual experience. I found out years later that was when they shaved the grass and planted all the winter flowers. So it wasn't a spiritual experience, it was what happens every year in the desert. But it changed my attitude and I thought there must be a God if he could make it look that beautiful. I think that was a big deal for me.

I ended up staying in the desert for a few years. I was on my Ninth Step and everybody kept telling me I needed to make amends. My mom called and said, "Can you come help at the travel agency?" I wanted to say no. But I was on my Ninth Step and I really wasn't allowed to say no. So I went thinking I was going to be up there for six weeks. I ended up there for nineteen years. Now I'm back in the desert.

I did a lot of Danny and Helen's trips. I did their trips and they went with me on a lot of trips. They were with me on a sober cruise in Alaska, and also with me in Hawaii. They were a very integral part of my sobriety as was Bill and you. You probably don't know it but I watched you a lot.

I had been in so many rehabs that were like hospital kind of settings. They were always telling me it was my childhood issues. That if I could get past my childhood issues, then I could get sober. I would tell them no, I don't think it's that, I think it's that I drink too much. We would battle, and because I was young they would tell me I had to be a drug addict. I would tell them, "No, no, no I'm really not, I'm just an alcoholic." I would readily admit I was an alcoholic. They would fight me that I was a drug addict because of my age. I told them to look at my toxicology reports. I don't do drugs. They would tell me I was in denial.

When I got to the club, within ten minutes talking to Danny, he never said anything when I told him I was only an alcoholic. I could tell he knew. I could tell he hadn't gone to school for psychology. He was an alcoholic. There was something different. I believe it was just one drunk talking to another. It was totally unique in all the rehabs I had been in.

Before I got sober, I was drinking one night and staying at my parents house. The next morning my dad was furious because I had been drinking. I was trying to talk to him and he was standing at the stove in the kitchen and he had his back to me. My dad is really nice; easy going. I said, "You know this guy cut me off on the freeway and he's such an asshole, and this girl said something to me and she's such an asshole." I went on and on like that for a few minutes and my dad wheeled around and he had a spatula in his hand. He started pointing the spatula at me.

He said, "You know Laurie every time you drink the whole world becomes an asshole. Did you ever figure that out?" He turned around and had his back to me. I thought 'well you're an asshole too.'

Within a year later I'm walking in the ABC Club and I had barely got in the door. Danny says, "You know you're an asshole and the most you'll ever be is a sober asshole." Because he used the same word that my Dad had, I believed him. I knew he was right. That made a big impression on me.

I think I had between one and three months. That was when Danny quit smoking and he decided he was going to get healthy. The whole club had to go for a walk every night. So there we were going for a walk and he turned to me, out of the blue and said to me, "You know you are really sick."

I said to him, "Well kiss my ass, you're really sick too." Thinking he meant sick in the head as a joke.

He looked at me and said, "No I don't think you understand. Seriously, you are really sick." And he meant physically. That was the truth. It also was the best I'd felt in six years. That's how bad I was and that was the day I realized how bad I really was. I was only twenty-five. I had been told that I had liver damage at twenty-three. Bad liver damage. I've never had any problem with it since I've been sober.

I loved going to Fellowship Hall in the mornings because it was all those old men that were just alcoholics. They weren't ever trying to be anything else. I related. That's why I have a difficult time when I go to a meeting and everybody is identifying as an alcoholic/addict. If all you identify as is alcoholic/addict I have nowhere to go.

When I lived in the club I became friends with Stephanie and Teresa. They were both heroin addicts. So we did a deal were every other Saturday night we would go to the Saturday AA Meeting, and every other Saturday we would go to a NA Meeting. I would identify as an addict in NA, and they would identify as alcoholics in the AA Meeting. Because of that and the book study's Danny did at the club, I know more about NA than most of the people that tell me they go to NA.

There were lots of us that got sober within two weeks of each other. Many others came in the club, but after two years there were only four of us left. When we had seven years of sobriety I was at the International Convention in Minneapolis. Stephanie called me to tell me that Teresa had committed suicide. How could she do that? Didn't she know how painful it was for the people left. The following Valentine's Day Stephanie committed suicide.

The only two left of us who got sober is me and Tom S. He has four more days then me. We used to take our cakes together, and now that I'm here maybe we can again.

Karen F

My sober date was August 19, 1987. Still is. I got sober in Palm Desert. I'm one of those people who basically walked in off the street. I went to one meeting in July of 1987 and because I was going for someone else, and subsequently I went on the 18th of August, but I had been up all night so I started on the 19th of August. I heard about the ABC Club. I don't even remember how, cause I was a little foggy.

My first introduction to the ABC Club was by a women named Diane G. She was my sponsor then, and my first sponsor. She had me meet her at the Thursday Night Women's Meeting. It was in the old house, the old main building, upstairs. Helen was there and I was so amazed that Helen was so kind, and she was sober. Diane was so wonderful to me. She just sort of let me snuggle up because I was so broken. That was when I found the ABC Club. I realized that it was a safe place to go to during the day. So I would go for noon meetings and that's when I started seeing Danny. My sponsor moved around November 1987 and I went to her sponsor, and that was Jeanie Theodore, She passed away a few years ago.

Every Friday night Jeanie, Nick, and a bunch of us would go out to dinner, and we would go to the ABC Club meeting. I would go during the week to meetings. Sometimes Danny and Helen would let me just come in and sit, because I needed somewhere just to sit, and know I was going to be okay. Even though I lived all the way in Palm Desert. Friday night we would go to meetings, together, all of us, and that's were I started feeling safe at the ABC Club. And finding out about AA and my family. Danny and Helen and Jeanie and Nick were my family and they helped raise me, and taught me all I needed.

Danny used to tell me, "You can do anything." He would smile at me and there was this knowing that he had and I had no idea.

In 1992 I had gone back to school to community college and I was cleaning houses because I couldn't go back to any of my old jobs. After I got sober I was basically unemployable. I started cleaning houses, and then I went to college. And I started going to law school and I ended up being a clerk at the public defenders office. I would call Danny and say, "Danny, Danny I got this guy."

He'd say, "Oh, bring him over." And I'd send them over there. Of course lots of time they weren't done and he would call me and say, "Come and get him."

I'd say, "What do you want me to do with him? Kick him out if you need to."

So we got this rapport, and to have a working relationship, and he was in the courts and he helped a lot of people, a lot of guys, a lot of women. I could send them to the club. That was before the baby Doll House and the new house. It was still real basic. That was in the early 90's.

Then I ended up leaving the desert in '97. I came back to Carlsbad in '99 and I would go out to the desert and speak and go and see Danny. I spoke at the breakfast meetings a lot. Danny and Helen were always there.

Then Helen was starting to get sick and Danny and I would talk on the phone occasionally, just so he could talk about it and what was happening.

Jeanie passed away and it was the hardest thing I ever had to go through. Not having my sponsor and I moved back from Carlsbad. Part of it was to be close to her so I could drive over to the desert to see her. Because by then she was in her bed all the time. When she died the memorial service was at the club. I'll never forget it. Danny had this chair he always sat in. It had armrests. Sort of looked like the king's chair. I thought of it as a little throne. It was up in front at the memorial service. I walked in and Danny said to me, "Karen you can sit in this chair today." He used to tell me I was his hero and he always told me everything was going to be alright. There are people in Alcoholics Anonymous that are my hero's and he was one of mine. The bond we had was really clear. That he knew that I was going to be okay, no matter what. I went through a lot of really hard things in sobriety and he was there.

The last time I saw him was at the last breakfast meeting that I spoke at, and we had a chance to talk. And again he told me, "Your my hero." I used to smile and laugh and tell him how much I loved him. The gift he gave to people was his clarity and his honesty. Helen brought a love and a softness. They balanced each other out. That was what was so remarkable.

I knew sometimes people were afraid of Danny, but I knew who was underneath. I believe Danny gave me the chance to know him as he truly was. I am so grateful that I had that opportunity.

I am now laid off from the state of California after spending ten years as a parole judge, with the Board of Parole Hearings. I just opened a small criminal defense office. I'm currently co-writing a book. I'm going to take a flower arranging course class to help work with my daughter who now has a Culinary Arts Degree, and I am also a grandma. I have my grandson. I'm still an active member of Alcoholics Anonymous. Sponsoring, being sponsored. Getting my moneys worth out of an incredible life that's been given to me. I'll be twenty-seven-years sober in August.

Tim H

I showed up the first time in '87. Just come off of a three day run. Was coming down, and I went to my mom's house. I knocked on her door, she answered, I told her I had a drug problem. She called the church and I went up and had a interview with the pastor. The pastor of my church called the ABC Club. I was there for six months.

The second time I was there ten months.

The third time I was there for sixty days.

The fourth time they detoxed me and sent me somewhere else. That was in '94. I've been sober since then.

Danny and Helen and my relationship was very personal. I did a lot of work painting and remodeling their home, twice, so I got to see them interact.

You can't beat Danny and Helen. They are lifesavers. My relationship is to love them. They were always there for me. No matter what they never turned me down. Every time I went down there for help they helped me. That's why I'm here now. They never gave up on me. I love them to death.

This is making me emotional. When he was leaving. If it wasn't for Danny letting us know every time we got in his face, while he was still at the club, and all that was going on you could see it in his eyes. He'd tell us I'm okay, I'm alright. If he would have said the wrong thing the ABC Club wouldn't exist now.

I loved the PYSM. That is what gave me what I needed for me to stay sober.

I showed up this last time in the PYSM, I usually sit real close to each one of them whatever they're doing. He looked at me and he said two things to me. He said, "Look at you, you're getting sicker." The other thing that he said to me that really screwed me up, he said, "Oh I heard you were working for your drugs." At that moment when he said that to me, I never felt that low when I was out there drinking and drugging. They sent me to this work ranch. Every time I wanted to leave I would think of what he said to me. That I was working for my drugs. I would change that around to, I was working for my recovery.

I was the disc jockey for all the dances at the ABC Club since '87. New Years Eve I was the DJ for eight years in a row.

I now work doing just about everything construction wise, and sponsor a living sober house in Desert Hot Springs. I've been doing that for seventeen years. It's tearing my pocket up. Most of the girls that come to it right now are from the House of Hope. I take them in and support them while they go get a job and start working. Maybe thirty percent of them I get my money back and the rest of them I don't. I keep the door open. It costs me $1,500 a month just to keep the house open. It's in Desert Hot Springs.

Tiffany H

I was young when I first went to the ABC Club. I lived with my grandparents. My grandpa, Bill, worked there. My grandma and I would come visit and eat dinner with him on Friday nights. Due to my age of six-years-old I don't recall meeting Danny. I do remember I saw Danny as my second grandfather. He would ask me how I was doing, what my grades in school were, and tell me how smart I am and for me to always do good.

Helen was very nice. She had a lot of dolls. Same as Danny, she would ask me how I was doing.

The club was good to me, and after a while when my mother went into sober living. I was allowed to live there. I was able to run around and do almost what ever I wanted to at the club.

The annual barbecues were great. Halloween and all the holidays were kid friendly.

So I was hanging around there from six to thirteen years of age. We moved when I was thirteen.

Now I'm sober. I went through the Ranch Recovery home, but I was raised at the ABC Club. I have two beautiful daughters. and my life is good.

Glenn W

I got to the ABC Club August 12, 1993. I got there because I was manufacturing meth. I was in jail with others, who were there for other reasons. They told me they were on their way to prison, but that I had never been to recovery. If I wanted to try recovery to start writing the ABC Club once a week telling them that I would like to try recovery. That is how I got in there.

I was a resident and most of all my relationship with Danny and Helen was going to meetings, and doing what I was supposed to do.

I was in recovery for seven months and in sober living for four months. The most interesting part of it was the Tuesday night PYSM. My favorite would be recreations and interacting with the other residents. Soft ball games, bowling, and stuff of that sort. My worse was the meeting where you were in the hot seat and everybody told you what your shortcomings were. I didn't like that too much. I like it now, but not then.

I never got to sit down with Helen, and talk to her, and get to know her better.

I never really spoke to Danny about how he felt about me when I got there, but I stayed in touch with him up until the day he died. He was very proud of me and what I had accomplished and he was very, very happy I stayed clean and sober in my first try at recovery.

The whole time I was using my wife was very distant. She has always been what we call a 'normy' and she was devastated when this all happened. She knew I was drinking, but she had no idea I was using meth. When it happened she made the decision to give me a chance to recover. We got some help, and we saved our house that we had. When I got out of the club I went back to the same house. Started working for a company, moved up rapidly with this company, doing what I had always done, marble and granite. I became a superintendent and pretty soon I was in charge of seven employees. Soon I decided to open my own company. We ended up selling the house in La Quinta. We moved to Bermuda Dunes. I told my employer that I wanted to try to open my own company and he was all for that. He knew where I had come from and he wished me the best. He said if ever I wanted a job, to come on back.

I opened my own company in 2006 and that's what I've been doing ever since. We made it through the recession and we're going good now.

Traci N

I got to the club April 3, 1999. Oh my God I was dying. Betty Ford Center determined I needed long term treatment. They knew their twenty eight day program wasn't going to do enough for me. They forced me to get on the ABC waiting list and that saved my life. Before I got there I spent another thirty days drinking. I hit that place where I called the club and said, "I got to come in." They said they didn't have room. I said, "I've got to come in. I can't do this anymore." For the first time I said that, and they said okay come in.

My first experience with Danny was the night I got there. Showed up around five o'clock Friday night. I asked him if I could use the phone to call my mom.

He said, "Your on probation." You know Danny, he was grumpy. Scared the Hell out of me.

"I've got to tell my mom I'm here. So she knows that I'm here."

"Make it quick."

Right there I knew to stay away from Danny. Someone I knew to stay away from and I did for a very long time. Helen I didn't have much interaction with.

My second week there I knew right away that the one thing you didn't want was your name called. He called my name after the weekend. My heart dropped and I thought 'What did I do?' He forbid me to go to the car washes. I had gone to my first car wash. I had came in the club yellow, and I came back from the car wash bright red.

He said, "You are forbidden to go to the car wash again, because if you die out there they are not bringing back your body."

I stayed for two and a half years. Thirteen months in-patient and a year and a half in sober living. I think I did it mostly by staying out of the way. Doing what they told me to do. A lot of my interaction was with the other staff members; the women there. Helen scared me. Unfortunately it wasn't until I got out and had some sobriety that I warmed up more to her. I saw her going to meetings and that. I knew Danny and Helen could control staying there, or not. I knew if I left I would die. That's after two months when I was supposed to leave. I truly believed if I left I would die. I got lucky. Right before the end of my time I was crying.

Tony S said, "What are you worried about ?"

I said, "I can't leave, I can't leave

"Trust God, trust God."

"But you don't understand."

"Trust God."

Then right before I got ready to leave they found me a county bed and I could stay.

The whole thing saved my life. The whole program. The meetings. I had done meetings before, but it wasn't until we had as many meetings as we did and it really started sinking in how it had to be. The alumni, the people that came to the club, because of what they got there, and what they showed us. It was amazing how it was, and what they had built up, and stories of how it came to be.

At six months of sobriety I had a run in with Bill. I was walking and he looked at me and said, "Why aren't you working yet? You should be working now."

I was still really sick and weak at that point. That was my encounter with him so I stayed away from him too.

I guess my sponsor said, "She's not here that long, so leave her be."

I guess I got lucky staying there that long. I did work here and there. When I was nine months sober I got the job I have now. I've been there coming up on fifteen years. It was because another alumnus called the club looking for a little bit of help and now, there I am.

When they transitioned from the old sober living into the new ones they kind of forgot that I'd been in the other ones so I got to stay another year instead of the six months. It was that last six months there that I determined I could do this. I'm ready to go. It saved my life. Even all the groups and stuff you don't think of, a little bit of CODA and all the funny ones. It was the way they put it all together. It wasn't just getting clean, it was learning how to live life, how to live the program. How to do it all.

Steve M

I'm going to share my experience at the ABC Club with Danny Leahy. I went there on 12/12/00. I pulled up in a dump truck with all my belongings, after being evicted from my apartment, where I refused to leave. I had everything in my dump truck, and I still remained in my abandoned apartment. Sneaking into a broken window for sometime until finally the sheriffs were staked out in front of the apartment. I was totally, completely unable to stay there, and I had to do something.

At which time I got my dump truck and pulled into the ABC Club with all my belongings in the back of it, and asked Danny if I could get sober there. I was financially strapped at the time. I was unable to pay for my recovery. He said he would like my truck for my recovery.

I said, "No, all my stuff is in my truck. That's where I'm currently holding my belongings."

He said, "Well, get your shit out of my truck."

I was at a crossroads right then and there. I had to get rid of all my stuff and I didn't have a place for all my stuff, and didn't have money to buy a storage unit. I knew I had to start a restart button, and start my life all over again. I didn't really have anything of extreme value, and it would be okay to just lose everything, and start all over again. So I took my dump truck to the Indio Swap Meet. I hit my power takeoff button, which is the dump truck button, that lifts up the bed, and proceeded to pour all my stuff out onto a fifteen by twenty square that I rented at that Saturday afternoon swap meet. To put for sell everything. You would be surprised when you want to get rid of stuff how fast it goes. My prices were very reasonable because I had no place for the stuff. Three to five dollars. Everything went.

I brought my truck into Danny Leahy at the ABC Club where he used it to get donations, and dump runs, and stuff. He constructively used it while I stayed there. He gave me a job title there also, for a while, driving my dump truck around which he currently owned. It gave me a sense of responsibly, a sense of security too, and worked to my benefit which was nice. More importantly it gave me a restart in life. It's so hard, I think, to let go of everything, and restart over. It is required sometimes in sobriety. Complete life change of sobriety. To change everything. We always want to hold onto this idea and that idea.

For me, I had to change everything. I needed to change my career. I needed to change my sobriety date. A new identity, new friends and playmates, and new play places. That's what Danny Leahy and the ABC Club facilitates. So important in recovery.

So I went there. I had to get a new job, a new career, and all new friends. For my year there that's what took place.

In my early recovery I would stay just past my probation period, ninety days, I was able to leave the house now. I was able to get a fellow ABC'er recovery person to go with me to my house to do some work for my mother. The guy who I chose decided to take some personal items from my mother, at the time we were doing some work. He stole some $5,000 diamond earrings. I didn't know this. We were there to run some cable for the television. He had decided to take some personal items. I was not aware of this, but quickly after we left my mom realized the diamond earrings were gone. She realized that only me and this person were there. She proceeded to think it was me. She called the ABC Club and said I was there burglarizing my mom. Taking advantage of her while I was there on my first stint of leaving the recovery house. Here everything I had on getting sober, and had given my dump truck, and started fresh, was almost pulled out from underneath me.

My whole everything was in Danny's hands. My mom was convinced I ripped her off again. I was trying to convince Danny that this was not the case. I had given everything I owned to be here for the last three months. I honestly had no idea what happened. I was not involved in the conspiracy, nor did I do it. The person that did it quickly left the club. That's how I pieced it together. I believe that on that day Danny believed me. He believed me that I would not do this. I will always be grateful that he believed in me that day.

I did change my sobriety date three years later, but never the less I did change my life that day. I've continued down the road of sobriety ever since that day. I had a break in my sobriety, but nevertheless I've continually been involved in the program. Sober today with double digit sobriety. Even though it took me a couple of times to get it, I've got it today. One day at a time I will continue to have it.

For those years in early 2000 in my stay in the ABC Club I will be forever grateful.

Clarence O

My sobriety date is 5/1/1999. I arrived at the ABC Club. I don't know how, or where they picked me up, but I got picked up by the Indio Police Department. I was homeless prior to that. Instead of going to jail they took me to the detox center at the ABC Club. From there I left the property. I was afraid of everything that was going on there, and afraid of the people looking at me. I left and for some reason that was my surrender. I walked around the block and back to the club and sat down where I started. That was the beginning of my recovery.

I stayed in the detox center for about a month. There was two detox managers at the time, Tony S and Roger Minton. They would take turns. God was there with me from day one because I was only allowed there for five days. For some reason I ended up staying there thirty days in detox. They were offering me recovery in Blythe. I didn't know nothing about recovery. I kept telling them to just give me one more day. That day added on to thirty days.

From there, there was a bed ready upstairs. I didn't realize how hard it was to get in the program. Going upstairs my idea was to rest. It was quite the opposite. Once I got upstairs I had to do a lot of meetings every day. It was good for us there. We needed to stay out of our heads. There was no chance of resting. It was meetings, meetings, meetings. They drilled that into us. That's exactly what I needed. For a person who didn't want to be there, I ended up staying there two months shy of five years.

I got my foundation there. I got my sponsor there. There was a group there that I remember real well that helped me change my life. It's on a Wednesday and called the Weekly Recovery Plan. It was things we wanted to do; to take care of that week. For some reason this girl called me out on my shit 'cause I kept putting the same thing down, and I never did anything. I wish I could remember her name. If it wasn't for that girl that called me out on my stuff I wouldn't be where I am today. I really believe that helped. I kept putting down that I was going to get my driver's license. That I was going to take the test. I was a procrastinator. I would say that every week and she caught on to me. She asked me what I was going to do after the meeting. I had no good answer for her. She said she would walk me to the office and get me a house driver, and see to it that I would get a ride to DMV, to see about my driver's license. That was the beginning of good things to come. If it wasn't for her I would not have done it.

I got a house driver. They took me to DMV. I took my test and passed. They gave me my temporary license and a couple of weeks later they sent me my driver's license. I was a house driver for Danny Leahy, and I got to take my peers there to outside meetings Fridays and Mondays. That didn't last long. A couple of weeks later I got a letter saying they garnished my driver's license because of child support. That was the first time in recovery I got the case of the fuckits. I wanted to give up. It all started to come to me.

Now I know how I became homeless were I ended up in the desert. It was all because I was running away from responsibilities. I completely forgot all about that. When they took my driver's license away I wanted to give up. I said, "What's the use?" If it wasn't for the staff there telling me to do the next indicated step I would have run. That's all I know how to do, is run. I don't know how to live.

I thought I had an alcoholic and drug problem, but it was actually a living problem. I learned all that at the club. So I did what was suggested from my peers and staff members there. They told me to pay the child support. So we got a plan and they started taking $25 a week from my check. That was fine. A month later they raised it up to $50. I went to talk to staff and they said, "Just pay them." So I did what they said and I kept paying it and paying it. It ended up going up to $700 a month. By that time I had already learned that that was the right thing to do. I had to clear the wreckage of the past.

I thought it was just getting clean and sober, but it was a whole lot of work. I ended up paying all my child support through the grace of God and the help of the staff members at the ABC Club. I think the total was $47,000 I had to pay. I got that out of the way and I had some other bills I had to pay. Hospital bills that I didn't know about, and court fines. I ended up paying it all. It was by the grace of God and the people that were patient enough to teach me how to live. I didn't know how to live. I knew nothing about recovery. I thought it was a cult. I was afraid of everybody there. I had this huge wall around me and I didn't want anyone to know me. Slowly I started tearing it down and that's when people started getting close to me and helping me out.

Danny and Helen were a big part of my life. In the beginning I didn't know who Danny was. I didn't like Danny. He was a real strict man. But I learned how to love that man. He became a father figure to me, and Helen a mother figure and I will forever be grateful for them. They were patient enough to teach me how to live.

I started working for Danny Leahy. I was a house driver. Then they started the Leather Plus store. We started in North Indio in a storage facility. From there we moved to the first little store on Oasis Street. I started moving furniture around and picking up donations. One day led to a month, and a month led to a year. I started saving up money, and I got my first little truck. I just kept going. I never thought I'd be where I'm at today. This ABC Recovery Center's been a blessing in my life.

I have three daughters and my middle age daughter came and found me there. She found out her dad was in recovery. She was seven years old when her mother and I divorced. When she found me at the ABC Club she was eighteen years old and had a little girl in her arms. We talked a couple of hours on the property there. When she left I went back to my room and I started packing up my suitcase. I was going to run again. I had already got this sobriety and a little bit of recovery and I knew nothing about being a father, or a grandfather. My head wanted to run because that is what I do best. Run from responsibilities.

I went to bed, and I woke up still there. I prayed about it and the obsession to leave was gone. Thank God I didn't run again. I would have missed it all. To this day I have a great relationship with my daughters. I have four grandkids. I went to see one yesterday playing baseball. He's in the all stars. He hit a home run and that was great. I have it on video. There is just so much in life that I would have missed if I would have ran.

My life has been so amazing, and this is just the beginning for me.

Today I work in the Laborer's Union. My sponsor is in the union. I talked to him ten years ago and told him I used to be in the Laborer's Union when I was married. When I was a lot younger. He suggested I go see about getting back into it. So I went over there and they had this apprenticeship program. I had to start all over and I joined the union. That's what I do. I'm a worker. It's a good paying job. I love what I'm doing. It's allowed me not only to live from paycheck to paycheck, but to save money.

I bought my first home last year. My very first home. I treasure that. It was something that was not even in my sight. The gifts just keep coming. We can do anything we want if we put our minds to it once we get clean and sober. I didn't graduate high school so I didn't think I could get to far in life. It's quite the opposite. We alcoholics and addicts are smart people. We have to learn how to keep stuff. I'm invested in the union. I have twelve years invested. I'm looking for another good five years. I'll be comfortable with my retirement from the union. If I'm able to work longer than that it will be fine. I love to work

I'm fifty two years old now. I know I wasted a lot of good years and my health. I'm in pretty good health today now that I don't use or drink. I know I can do it. I was taught to suit up and show up, and be on time. I'm never late; I'm always early. I do a lot of out of town work. I'm really active with my grandchildren and that is what I live for today. I understand this is for me first, but they're a motivating factor for me. I've been blessed with a second chance at life.

Tommy A

I met Danny in the late 80's, early 90's. I met him through my brother. My mom was having trouble with my brother. My brother hit an electrical telephone pole with his car and almost killed himself. My mom went to see Danny about getting him in the club. She was able to get him in the club for a minimum fee. The miracle of Danny was he got a lot of people through the club without money. A lot of people got sober.

I heard a lot about him before I got to meet him. How much everybody liked him and had such respect for him. I went there and looked in the room. I didn't want to get sober, but I found out about sobriety through that. Eventually I would get sober by myself. I would start going to the ABC Club by myself and wanting to hang around Danny and I fell in love with him, and who he was. I wanted to be like him someday which is hard shoes to fill.

He loved everybody and he never said no. I heard him say no when people took advantage of him. I never heard him say no when people asked him, with pain. After that if you did what you did and were disrespectful to him he would let you go, but he always gave you the opportunity. I thought that was the best of Danny, to always give you the opportunity.

What happened is we didn't have any money to give Danny. We were struggling. Even though we had been in business for a long time we struggled to survive. So what we did is do work for the club. The first thing we did was paving the parking lot in front of the mess hall. That is the old house to me. That's where I started going to meetings. I know the other one in the back is the original old house. We paved the front with a concrete parking lot. My mom really loved Danny. Whatever we could do for him we did. We bartered with Danny to get my brother, and one of my cousins in there. Whatever we could do to get people in there. We did a lot of work at the club. That's how I found out about Danny Leahy and the club.

My brother was getting sober, my dad was getting sober, so I started kicking around this idea in my head of getting sober. I ended up going to the club, and started going on walks with Danny after the Tuesday

Night Chip Meeting, and Friday Night Speaker Meeting. I'd hear all about Danny kicking people out, but he wasn't like that to me. He showed me incredible respect. He talked to me like a friend. He never had to tell me not to mess with the girls, he never had to tell me all that other stuff, because I heard him tell other people. He always took a kind and liking to me. Every time he saw me he would say, "Tommy come sit with me." I felt really special.

I got to go with him one time when he spoke in Riverside. I heard him speak on a tape once, but I never really heard him. Some times it wasn't clear, or I didn't understand what he said. But that one time in Riverside he spoke at a men's banquet. It was the best thing and he spoke so clear. I finally got his message. I could feel his pain over his family, his relationship with his family. His kids and how he had put them on a shelf. It did take it's toll on him and Danny Junior's relationship. I could see the pain in Danny Jr. too. I think it's starting to wear itself off, for all the stuff we loved him for.

I spent time with him and Helen. Helen was happy, but I could tell she was sick. Nothing else mattered to him, he was there for her. He was committed. Everything else didn't matter any more.

Even when he died I was communicating with him. Going down to the Hacienda to see Danny. Two days before he died and he looked fantastic. He looked great, he was strong, he was doing exercises. I told him if he keeps doing like this I'll put you on the concrete crew. He laughed, and that was the last time I kissed him. That was the last time I saw him.

I loved getting sober. I got sober in 1991. I stayed sober just going to the club and anytime I could be around him by myself, I would be. We spent a lot of time together in San Felipe (men's retreat). It was a tremendous relationship with the respect that we had. Anytime he asked me to do anything for him, I would do it at the drop of a hat. I had that much respect.

My brother ended up going to the club two, or three times. My family had some problems and Danny would help them out. I got my wife's, who was my wife then, sister in the club. It was amazing what he was able to do. Everybody I know went through the club. Little did we know what we had was so special. It would never be like that again.

Things would change. I still go on Friday night, because it still has the magic of Danny.

I thought of that movie Custer. When they were ripping the stripes off of him. It reminded me of Danny. It was sad. I was on the board, and went to bat for him to get retirement, to give him $2,000 a month, but I got booted out of the board. At the end I was surprised at how many of Danny's friends voted me out. They sent the results to me.

Joe S

My name is Joe, here with Sunny and Bill. In 2005, April sometime
I paroled out of CRC (California Rehabilitation Center) at Norco.
February through SASCA (Substance Abuse Services Coordinating
Agency) I was given the opportunity to go to a place called the
Chapman House in Riverside. Of course that's right downtown and
I know everybody there, everybody knows me. On the west side, the
east side, downtown. I got dropped off. Within the hour I was getting
loaded.

I went upstairs to my room. Nobody was there for me to put my bags
away. I went back up about a half hour later and there was my roommate
getting ready to do a fix. No introduction just, "Hey you want some?"

Of course. First thing out of my mouth, "Yeah." So we did. That
started off bad from the get go. I was there two months. For the most
part loaded every day. Heroin is my drug of choice. On occasion I'd go
down to the corner with my home girls. They were in a motel there.
We'd smoke some speed, or something. At that for three, or four days.
Just wasn't done I guess. I was still doing what I did every time I got out
and got caught. One time they gave me a break, a chance. I told them
I won't do it again, of course I did. It wasn't long before they kicked
me out.

Two months into this they kicked me out. So I'm running around
downtown Riverside. I didn't want to do anymore crime. I'm a third
strike candidate. I hooked up with this lady who was doing what she
did in her addiction. I hung out with her about three weeks. I get mixed
up in my time frames. In April, must have been April 24th, 25th. I chose
April 26th. That's the day I got to the club.

Before that I was on the streets just getting loaded, getting loaded.
Once again I fucked up. I talked to my daughter. I talked to my son.
My son was cussing me out. My youngest boy. My daughter was asking
me, "Please dad just help me understand. Just why? Why again?" I had
no answers. I knew I had to do something, and something quick. I'd
pretty much burned out everybody. All my places. Didn't have nowhere
to go. The only place I knew I could go and be safe was at my moms. I
went to my mom's house. I went home.

Actually, what happened was I overdosed. I overdosed on a Saturday. Cops showed up. I'm on the corner of Second and Market at the Save a Minute store. I laid out in the middle of the parking lot. I came to. I didn't overdose, or I'd ended up in the hospital. I did a little too much and decided to laid down in the middle of the parking lot.

I don't remember getting there. I know we walked down the alley after we fixed. I guess I decided to lay down and nod out in the middle of the parking lot. Cops woke me up and searched me. Called my parole officer. My parole officer told them to let me go. If he doesn't have anything on him let him go and have him report to me, to call me Monday morning. That he had somewhere for me to go. Unknown to me. I didn't know it was the ABC Club.

That was a God shot. They told me to get out of here. To go find somewhere else to lay down. That they better not see me again, downtown. The girl down the street was waiting for me. We went back up to the motel room and I started having this moment of clarity. She put me in the tub. I lay in that tub thinking, once again I blew it, I messed up. I knew I had to do something different. I just didn't know what. I knew I had to get out of there, or I'd end up getting loaded again. Even after I'd gotten loaded too much already.

So I grabbed my stuff. I set on the steps of this church for about two hours. Starting to rain. I just flooded with all these emotions and wondering what my next move was gonna be. The best I could come up with was to go to my mom's. I'll go to mom's house, and I did. She wasn't there. I crawled into the tool shed, and was going to sleep for a while. She got home later on that night. She was out with my step dad and other family, my sister. I asked her if I could stay. She looked at me like she wasn't sure. I was always welcomed there. She was just tired of me living that way. She was tired of seeing me do this to myself. She let me stay. I always had a room in the back. I told her what happened.

Monday morning I called my parole officer and he said, "Do you want to go to prison? Back to prison, or do you want to try another rehab?" Of course I didn't want to go back to prison. He'd have to catch me 'cause I wasn't going back voluntary. They'd catch me eventually.

So I said, "Lets try the rehab." He told me to go to the ABC Club in Indio. I'd heard of the ABC Club before through the prison substance abuse program.

I said, "Ok, when?"

"Can you make it there by five o'clock today?"

I told him, "Sure." My mom called my son. My son got there right away. He picked me up. She gave him money for gas.

Gave me $20 and instructed my son, "Don't you dare stop anywhere." She knew I would spend that money on something.

He took me straight to the club. Dropped me off in front with two bags of clothes. I thought, I have arrived. That begin my journey. When I got there, there were two guys. One I knew well over thirty years. He was there doing detox. After a relapse of three years clean. He'd gone through the club. He knew Danny very well. Another guy named Johnny. They greeted me, "Hey what's up Joe, what's happening?" I didn't really want to talk to them. They said, "What are you doing here?" I wasn't happy to be here. Detox was rough. They threw me in detox for a week. Another home boy came by to see me, and he had like sixteen months clean at the time. He welcomed me to detox. He said, "You're here. What you going to do? What are you going to do different? Give yourself a break Joe. Just stay."

I didn't know what I wanted to do. I knew I had to do something different. Just didn't know what. Wasn't feeling very good. Physically I really tore myself up just running around in two weeks. That quick. I figured I'll get to feeling better and I'll run. I'll take off. That was the plan in the beginning. I did the detox, got up in the house upstairs. Still wasn't feeling good about a whole lot of things. Wasn't sure, skeptical about everything I was hearing. People laughing, smiling, and I didn't know what the Hell was so funny. People's smiles.

I seen this old man walking around. He'd never say anything to me. So about a month goes by. Finally one day I'm in the line for breakfast after the meeting, and he's looking at me. He walked past me in line, and he stops, and I'm looking at him. He turns around and says, "Come here asshole." I walked up to him. He goes, "Do you want to stay clean?"

I told him, "Yeah." Probably the dumbest look on my face.

"I'm going to tell you how to stay clean. I'm going to tell you how it's done. You trust God, clean house and help others."

I didn't have no idea what those words would mean to me as I started on my journey. I live by those words today. I walked away and those words, the longer I stuck around the more they meant to me. To this day they just do. I pass that on to my sponsees and I pass that on to newcomers. It was probably told to Danny some time ago. I don't know, but that formula seems to work for me, and countless others. I'm forever grateful for Danny and his staff. Bill W, and Bill M, and Helen of course. The old school stuff that was there then. My meetings today I still refer to it as Danny's house.

I stuck around and got to know Danny. Thank God I listened to him and I started following some directions. And in all the groups done by Danny and Helen during the week I started to listen. I needed to be told what to do. I really didn't have a problem with that. I'd been told what to do all my life. In prison I did what they told me to do. In his PYSM he'd do roll call. People would get kicked out. Danny would tell them, you don't need ABC to stay sober. Keep coming back to meetings. People would raise their hands and I'd always say, "I'm still here Danny and I'm grateful."

He'd say, "Well, you ought to be you asshole."

I was there eleven months. I did the primary care, and went across the street and SASCA paid for six months of it. Started working right away, as soon as thirty-five days restriction was over I was working. I had to surrender a little at a time. Still wasn't sure, even at forty-five days. I don't know how I'm going to do this. How's all these crazies going to keep me clean? I started with honesty, open minded and willingness. I'd hear all these cliques and it sounded like they were speaking Chinese. I didn't understand none of this.

I'd heard the program in prison, and just kind of winged it. I didn't pay attention to any of the stuff that was going on.

Somehow the seed was planted. The Serenity Prayer was huge. The only three words I got out of it was, I cannot change. I stuck with it for awhile. I kind of determined I was going to be a convict and a heroin addict the rest of my life. I was cool with that. Prison to me was in and out, in and out for the better part of thirty-seven years. Get out, get with the homies, get high and did crime. Sadly my kids came second. Wouldn't be long afterwards and I would be arrested again, with another charge most times. And I'm on my way back to prison. I was cool with that. I never gave much thought about life.

I did the program there. I started sharing. I started looking at the similarities and not the differences. We were all in the same boat. We're all, as Danny would say, a bunch of sickos trying to get better. I learned to love him and the staff there. Everybody there and the ABC Club. I don't call it the ABC Recovery Center, I call it the ABC Club still. So many people play a part in my recovery. Early on, and I'm so grateful today for that. Coming up on nine years in a couple of weeks. I trust God, clean house and help others. I have sponsees. Had a bunch of them, but not all of them stick around. I've got maybe six now that are doing the steps and being of service. Taking commitments and doing what I was taught to do. I walk them through the steps.

It's amazing if you stick around long enough to become honest. I had to get honest with you before I got honest with me, and anybody else. Thank God he told me, "Joe, give yourself a break. If you ain't happy in thirty days, give it a year. Give it thirty days first, then give it another month, then give it a year, and if you're not happy get the Hell out of here. Finish up. Go get done," Danny would say.

His last meeting out and about was at the Friday Night NA Meeting at the ABC Club. Danny sat right in front dropping his little oxygen tank making a bunch of noise. Nobody cared, nobody was going to say anything.

I was at his appreciation dinner at the Fantasy Springs casino. Got some of the coolest pictures.

Today I'm suiting up and showing up. I started working construction immediately after I got off restriction. I couldn't wait to get some money in my pockets. To be self supporting. I've been doing construction for years. I'm a maintenance man at a building we remodeled. I was working for the bosses dad before he died. The daughter told her dad that she was going to keep Joe for a while. And I'm still here. I keep the place up. I've been gainfully employed since I left the ABC Club.

I'm in my second relationship. My first I should have listened to Danny. It did not go well. My sobriety date is April 26, 2005. Danny was a big part of my recovery, Helen as well. As far as I'm concerned it's still Danny's House.

Beth L

I'm here with Sunny to tell a little bit of a story of how I got involved with the ABC Club in Indio. It started in 1990. I had been arrested and was in a world of trouble for some really crappy things that I had done. I was starting to go to meetings of Alcoholics Anonymous at the urging of my criminal defense attorney. I started going to meetings at Fellowship Hall. It wasn't very long after that that it was suggested I go down to this place called the ABC Club in Indio.

I needed to go down there and introduce myself and see if there was some volunteer work that I could do. I was very unemployable. There was a major possibility that I was going to have to go do some very serious prison time. The project really was to keep Beth out of prison. That's what the big goal was going to be. In about October, or November of 1990 I did go down to the club and immediately they had work for me to do. It was a lot of different things. It wasn't ever the same every day. I was very fortunate because I still had a drivers license and a car. There was a lot of people there that didn't have that, so that proved to be quite an asset to meet their needs.

I was still in a marriage, that wasn't going very well, to the alcoholic husband. I humiliated him by my actions. Nor could he understand why I had to go to those meetings. Why was I going down there with all those people down there in Indio, California? How could you even think about going down there and being with them? Spending your days there? You know they're lower companions. Little did he know, or realize how much I was enjoying myself. It was a place for me to go, to feel a part of. Another reason, big reason, was for me was to be around people that had gone to prison, or were going to go, or been in jail. Incarcerated someway, or other, so that I wouldn't feel so frightened about the whole thing.

I worked in the kitchen a lot. I did a lot of paperwork in the office. Did a lot of driving. They had what they called the bread run at that time. Were somebody would have to leave in a pickup truck and take a couple of people with you. Then we'd go to a couple of markets and pick up the day old bread and bring it back. Then there was always the residents that had to go up to Riverside General Hospital. So I was able to take the van. We would load the van up and take them up there, like every other week. I was lucky too because some days a week we were able to take the van, which is a big outing, to take the van to Fellowship Hall for the 7 a.m. meeting. We felt like this was a big privilege. It really was a big privilege.

I was really lucky, because when I got to the club I hadn't had anything to drink for about eight years. But I was not really truly sober. I had a lot of untreated alcoholism. I had inappropriate behavior with a lot of anger issues going on. A lot of that kind of started to subside the more I could be around these people who had become my friends. Actually these were, believe it or not, people I could trust even though they had pasts that were not perfect either.

I had to go to court a lot, I was in court an awful lot. That was just for things that had to get taken care of, and it was a long drawn out process. At the same time I was in the midst of trying to get a divorce. That wasn't going very smoothly either. Then in July of 1991 was a couple of big days. I was in court, and they read this whole thing out about everything. All this stuff I had done. I had been involved in a situation in town. It was a big news deal on KESQ TV, and The Desert Sun, and all of my dirty laundry had been aired out. On television, and in the newspaper, and everything. Danny Leahy became really good at keeping the television sets off during the news when Beth had been to court. Because it was a disruption in the house. The residents were curious, but I was so ashamed and embarrassed that I just couldn't deal with it. There came a time when the television sets were just turned off, and we didn't have to go through that.

Later on that month I was back in court for sentencing and much to my surprise, I had no idea this was going on, I was kept outside of the court room for quite some time. My attorney was with me and he said we had to wait outside for a while. The more we had to wait, the more afraid I became. What are they going to do to me? Where am I going to go? Where am I going to be? Am I going back to the club tonight? What's going to happen to me? Ironically they had to clear out all the seats in the court room, because there wasn't enough seating for friends of mine, that really cared about me, and residents from the club had somehow, or other figured out a way to get over there to that court room.

Even to this day it's an emotional deal to really understand how much I was really cared for. At home I was not getting that message. I was getting a totally opposite message. So to get that message there was emotional. It all turned out well. I wasn't sent away to any kind of prison. Instead I got a bunch of probation and then I moved into the club, and had a bed there. I had been told a couple of months before that anytime I was ready to leave that marriage there would be a bed waiting for me. And there was. We didn't have to make a big deal. I'm ready to move. I'm going to make the move.

It was very hard for me to do. I left, and walked out of my home and a twenty year marriage. I left behind everything. My sponsor told me to take a hundred dollars, and as much clothes as I could put in my car and back down the driveway, and don't even look out your rear view mirror, because you're never, ever, going to see that life again. I'm kind of a nester. I like my home. I like my things. I'm like that. It was really, really hard. A lot of tears were shed over that. I got the comfort at the club that I could get no place else. My new friends in AA told me you've got to suit up and show up Beth. Everything is going to turn out okay. Suit up, show up, and keep turning it over. I kept hearing those three things over, and over, and over again.

Things did turn out. Danny and Helen allowed me to stay at the club as long as I wanted to. I spent a lot of hours there doing community service work that was all kept track of which was two fold. I was doing them a really big favor, because they didn't have to hire somebody to do what I was doing for them. By the same token I was able to collect all these community service hours. About half way through probation, again, Danny took me to court. I was taken off probation at the half way mark. I gave the court back four thousand hours of community service time. At the same time, my felonies were all dropped to misdemeanors. It turned out that a really good friend of mine whose husband was the DA on the case would be in court the same day I was there. It was a funny situation, but anyway it all worked out. I doubt that anybody gave a rat's ass about what was going on.

I'm just eternally grateful. After some time, in 1992, I left the club and started a new life with somebody else, but continued to be of maximum service that I could to the ABC Club. They gave me a home when I had no place else to go. I will never forget those days. I loved it. I loved my time there. Yeah, there were things that would drive you crazy. The noisy chairs, the noisy people, people screaming, the girls staying up until eleven, twelve at night. I'd be exhausted and the girls coming in my room saying, "Could we talk to you?" I wouldn't trade some of that. Teaching girls how to do laundry. They'd never done laundry before in their life. It blew me away that they didn't even know you had to separate the whites, from the colored. It was fun. I felt like a mother to a lot of the girls. I was probably old enough to be their mother if the truth was known.

After getting out we got the alumni really rolling along, and we did a lot of fun things with it. A lot of activities. I loved seeing people having such a good time, sober. They could bring all of their family to these events and just enjoy themselves. In a way I was happy to move out. It was time to move out and get a life of my own, but I will forever be grateful. I feel sad lots of times that the ABC Club is not anywhere near like it was in those days. Things change and we have to accept that that's the way it is as sad as it can be. I'm so grateful I'm sober and so eternally grateful for the opportunity. I wouldn't trade it for anything.

Dana M

Memories of Danny and Helen

In my first few months of sobriety, outside my treatment center, the 7 a.m. Attitude Adjustment at Fellowship Hall was the first meeting I attended. It eventually became my home group, in early sobriety anyway. That is where I was first introduced to Danny Leahy. An older man to me, a little over twenty years my senior, slightly balding with twinkle eyes, he might just be another face in the crowd except when he walked into the meeting, others took note.

Danny always started his share the same way, "I'm not an authority on anything. I don't claim to be. I didn't come here to win friends, or influence people...." All attention was on him when he spoke, not because of his stutter, but because he did have an influence on everyone in the meeting. I'd soon find out he was the director of the ABC Club in Indio. "In Indio, really? Who cares?" I'd think to myself as I sat on the curb and looked down upon others. After all, I came through the doors from a nationally acclaimed treatment center in Rancho Mirage. There was no mistake that this man who endearingly referred to a person he loved as asshole had a presence of adoration and respect. "Indio, really?" As a newcomer, I thought that affluence and fame were important traits to strive for but I was intrigued to know how this little old guy who ran a halfway house in Indio was revered by so many.

Rarely would you hear about Danny without knowing he was married to Helen. She was somewhat of an enigma as she was not the socialite that Danny was. Hearing about Helen's Thursday night Women's Candlelight Meeting, my sister and I ventured down to the ABC Club to attend.

As we arrived to the old wooden house in Indio, we knocked at the front door. A gorgeous young man by the name of Chris answered the door. When we told him we were there for Helen's Candlelight Meeting, he told us her meeting was at her house around the corner. Then he flirtatiously invited us to come in and stay for the Men's Stag Meeting they were just going to start. Although he was not even twenty-one, my sister and I were like two schoolgirls, dazed in a dreamlike state

173

at Chris' charm (male model). As we drifted into the room he had to stop us, "This is a Men's Stag Meeting, no women allowed. To get to Helen's house you'll have to go out the back alley here, then make a right at the street. When you get to the corner, follow the next alley on the left and when you go through that, Helen and Danny's house are a few houses down on the right." Of course neither of us heard the directions precisely. Leaving the club, we drove around the neighborhood looking for alleyways and never found Helen's meeting.

The first time I saw Helen was after the new house at the club was built. It was the ABC Friday night Speaker Meeting. A few minutes before the meeting started. she walked into the filled hall to take her seat up front, saved by the residents. Helen didn't walk, she sauntered, as if the meeting would wait. I had always heard she was shy but I saw her as arrogant because the meeting would wait if ever need be until Helen arrived. Her presence intimidated me.

I had always heard it was Danny who intimidated the residents. And he did, it was typical to cower down to Danny, especially if you were up to no good and possibly breaking the house rules. Danny knew everything that was going on, he rarely missed a beat.

If a resident was shucking and jiving with other residents, or 'he-ing and 'she-ing' with each other he knew it, and a resident would avoid running into him at all costs. But when they did, he would give them the eye, sometimes snickering, "I know what you're up to." Some residents thought they could manipulate Danny by shucking and jiving with him, which never worked. They would still get the eye and snicker.

Now a good majority of the residents were following direction, abiding by the rules, working good programs, and willing to put their lives in order. They were the ones that were honored by Danny's endearing term, 'asshole.' Although confident and full of hope and faith, the alcoholic's biggest enemy is their ego. Danny would keep that in check by telling them, "I know you're doing great and that's really good, but don't forget where you came from. You're an asshole, just like me."

Danny didn't intimidate me that much, but Helen? She really intimidated me as she was so to herself and wouldn't say a lot. Any intimacy with Helen seemed impossible. Then again I was newly sober at that time and I thought I knew what intimacy was. I couldn't imagine years later, she would be my sponsor for twenty years. And it would be Helen who would teach me intimacy with my fellows, far beyond my expectations.

The second time I met Helen was at Sue Riley's Monday Women's Book Study. I wasn't more than a year sober. It was a small meeting with no more than twenty women, but again, hardly a peep from Helen. Her quiet disposition felt very untrusting to me. I could never get a read on what she was thinking, of me (of course), or anyone else in the room for that matter. I just had the impression she didn't like others all that much. I couldn't understand all the praise I would hear about Helen from other people, especially women.

I didn't see Helen for another year. She had suddenly and very unexpectedly left her post at the ABC Club. She had moved into a halfway house in Desert Hot Springs, not as a facilitator, but as a resident. Helen did not have a slip (fallen off the wagon), she had a breakdown of sorts. Not too many knew exactly why she took this reprieve in her life. Once again, true to her character, the mystery of what happened to Helen eluded me.

I was eighteen months sober when I experienced my first mental breakdown. I moved into Lost Heads Ranch who referred me to a six week co-dependency program at the treatment center I got sober in. There, I was given the mantra, 'depression is optional, you don't have to feel this way.' That got me through for a period. For the next six months although I was unemployable, I managed to keep working odd jobs in order to keep a roof over my head. The breakdown would subside for periods of time only to surface again and again.

By the time I was two years sober, I found myself holed up in the middle of the night at my sponsor's house, listening to Bobby E speaker tapes, a member of the fellowship who had fallen into the same predicament. My sponsor having to go to work the next day and not knowing what to do with me asked me where I think I should go. As divine intervention would have it, I replied, "I want to go see Helen Leahy." With that, my sponsor placed the call.

The next morning as luck, or God if you will, would have it a bed had just opened in the women's house. During my first meeting with Helen, I told her I would need to call in sick to my employer. She kindly advised me to be honest with them letting them know my situation and I would need to take a leave of absence. She sat right next to me and had me call and talk to them myself.

Helen gently told me her recent story on how some months back, she too woke up homicidal, too afraid to leave her home. I corrected her by saying, "Oh but they're one in the same. Homicidal is rage turned outward while suicidal is rage turned inward. Either way it's rage, and rage is extreme anger, and anger is fear."

"We're going to work on your fears while you're here." Thus began my journey with Helen.

On top of my women's meetings, I was introduced to ACOA (Alcoholic Children of Alcoholics) and CODA (Codependent Alcoholics) meetings while living at the club, but my favorite meeting of all was the mandatory resident meeting every Tuesday after dinner, Danny's Pack Your Shit Meeting. This is where Danny would call out any residents who were breaking house rules. The ABC Club was always overbooked with a long waiting list of alcoholics who were willing to do whatever it took for a chance at sobriety. Because of this there was no room for those who thought they could pull the wool over Danny's eyes and skate through their time at the club, many of who were sentenced by the courts.

At the beginning of the meeting and not at the end, Danny would stand up at the podium while all the residents stay quietly in their seats. He'd quietly gaze upon one particular guy, or girl. Then with a stutter he would say the person's name and tell them to "P-P-Pack your shit!" With that, the resident would get up from his (or her) chair, go directly to their room and pack their belongings. Anyway that was what was expected.

Quite often the resident would try to argue his case with Danny, or try to shuck and jive their way out of it, only to be drowned out by the laughter and howling of the other resident. Danny wouldn't have to say anything as it would be quickly apparent that Danny was not the only one aware of their shenanigans. Just as often all Danny would have to do is give them the look, and without saying a word the resident would scurry out of the hall before Danny could tell them to pack their shit. The best ones were the he-ing and she-ing. Danny would tell the guy to pack his shit and then immediately following he would look at the girl and that would send everyone in an uproar.

The next order of business was asking all the residents for the volunteer positions they would want to commit to for that week. There was always plenty to do beyond the daily chores, like working in the kitchen, babysitting for sober moms while they attended the meetings at the club, the monthly Alumni Speaker Pancake Breakfast, ad-infinitum. I worked out my own personal system. Every other weekend, I'd take a leave to spend time with my family, and every other weekend, I'd stay at the club for the Saturday Night ACOA Meeting. On the weekends I would leave, I'd volunteer to work at the alumni car wash. That way I would volunteer every week at Danny's house meeting.

The meeting would conclude with Danny handing out a small ceramic statue of a toilet, and each week a person would then be awarded the pity pot award. All of this might put a light of tyranny on Danny. The eyes in the back of his head and the humorous way he would deliver this tough love was anything but that. Keep in mind that on occasion, Danny himself would get the pity pot award.

I had been living at the club for a few months when my family intervened on me to seek psychiatric help. After meeting with the therapist my family sent me to, she turned me over to a psychiatrist who worked in her office. Within a half hour he was writing me a prescription for antidepressants. In those days to take a pill in AA was taboo and if you were to admit it in an open meeting, it would spark great controversy as to whether or not you should take a new sobriety anniversary date.

I went crazy for a moment, trying to emphasize this controversy to the good doctor. I was sobbing uncontrollably when trying to explain the rules of AA and, "I'm living in an AA recovery home. You don't get it! I can't take a pill to make me feel better." He called the club and got Helen on the line. After talking to her a bit, he handed me the receiver. I clearly recall Helen telling me, "You've been dual-diagnosed. Come home. We'll administer your antidepressants to you." A calm overcame me that I can only describe as a spiritual awakening.

Helen's words, "Come home," rang over and over to me. It sank in. I was home, then and for many years to come.

Upon leaving the club I asked Helen to sponsor me. She said she could not because as a CAADAC (California Association of Alcohol and Drug Abuse Counselor), her ethical guidelines would not permit her to sponsor any resident until they were out of her care for two years, or more. She told me however, "You know I'm here for you as a friend and you can call me if you ever need to talk." With that, I found a new sponsor while Helen and I remained friends.

My first year out of the club was still dicey. The sponsor who drove me to the club was not experienced with dual diagnosis. She was uncomfortable sponsoring me so I had to start with a new sponsor. I was in and out of depressive episodes, as I would choose to quit my antidepressants as prescribed.

About fourteen months out of the club, my new sponsor became unexpectedly busy and put off doing a Fifth Step with me until I let her go, about four months later. In the meantime, Helen kept her word and we met every Monday night for dinner before attending the Monday Night Women's Meeting.

While I was in therapy I was without a sponsor for about six months. During that time, when I would share in meetings, it was Helen's advice that I would refer to as my sponsor's advice. Finally when two years living out of the club had passed, I told Helen that when I would refer to my sponsor in meetings, she was who I had in my mind. "So it's okay that you're sponsoring me without you knowing it, right?"

She laughed and said, "I think the two years have passed so if I'm going to sponsor you, don't you think it's about time we did that Fifth Step you've been sitting on ?"

For the next twenty years, I worked the steps with Helen and learned so much. I've learned to set healthy boundaries with others. In AA we are taught to be as transparent as possible and some of us have no problem with that. Some of us can take such transparency to a fault. Helen would always tell me, "What you tell other people about yourself is on a need to know basis. And it's up to you and maybe another friend you trust what your need to know basis is."

Not that I always practiced doing this because I also learned that besides being alcoholic, I'm an ordinary human being. Not only did Helen teach me to be my fallible human self but she also showed me how to be fallible with grace. I might call her with a great idea of a boundary I many have to set with someone, or to run some letter of brutal honesty by her that I was intending on sending out. She would make suggestions on how to soften it up, or not to do it at all. I might reply with, "Oh no, I'm going to...but I have to..."

Helen would tell me, "Well, if it were me, this is what I would do, but you're not me and you're going to do what you want to do." She'd chuckle and say, "So whatever you decide to do, If you end up with egg on your face, you know I'll be here to help you wipe it off."

I remember one distinct lesson in learning to mind my own business, to detach, as the professionals would say. I was at a Saturday Night Speaker Meeting when the van from the club dropped a bunch of residents off for the meeting. I took my seat a row behind some of them. Midway through the meeting I saw a married male resident hold hands behind the seat with a single female resident. I couldn't wait for my Monday dinner with Helen so I could tell on them.

When Monday rolled around, I reported how I saw so-in-so with so-in-so he-ing and she-ing. "And don't you think Danny should be told, Helen?" I asked.

Helen rolled her eyes at me and said, "Alright, if they have something sexual, or romantic going on, are you going to get drunk over it?"

I replied, "No, I'm not going to get drunk." She chuckled at my being so appalled by this anyway.

"Besides," she said, "It was only a few years back when you came to me scared that Danny was going to ban you from the club for pining after a certain newcomer. Aren't you glad no one told on you?"

"I never acted out on that!" I argued. Helen chuckled some more and sarcastically said, "Yeah that's right, not under the wrath of Danny."

Helen had a very kind way of keeping me in check. Over the years she saw me through a lot in life, much of which is on a need-to-know basis. The lessons I have learned, the steps Helen had walked me through time, and again, how to live right sized, the thousands of pearls of wisdom are overwhelmingly infinite.

There was a prayer that use to hang in the main meeting hall at the club that went like this; <u>God if I can't have what I want today, please help me to want what I have.</u> Danny lived that prayer and it's probably the greatest lesson I learned from him, that and humility. I was an honor to be an asshole among assholes.

Some years later a few months after my husband was diagnosed with melanoma, Helen was diagnosed with lung cancer. Soon after, we moved to the beach to be closer to my husband's medical team. Helen survived my husband by two years. In the fall of 2008, when my husband was dying in the hospital, I remember whining to Helen, "I'm not ready to be a widowed single mom!"

And she calmly replied, "Yes, but God might be ready for you to be."

About three months before she passed, I hesitantly told her I should probably find a sponsor nearer to where I lived. She said, "God, I was wondering when you were ever going to get around to that."

I don't recall exactly when we spoke before she passed. It was during one of our holiday drives to the desert so I would guess somewhere before a month of her passing. I talked a bit, but cognizant of what little energy she had those days, I kept it brief, mostly telling her how grateful I was to have her in my life and how much I loved her. As she had so many times when we talked, she expressed her gratitude to have someone she could frankly admit to how she was ready to go. She always said, "I know you understand and I know it's okay to talk about these things." As always, expressing her gratitude.

I stayed in touch with Danny. A while after she passed, during a phone conversation, Danny gingerly announced he's ready to start dating and find some one else to settle down with. "Danny! How could you?" I exclaimed, "Helen hasn't even been gone six months." He very matter-of-factly told me, "Mary Helen told me to. She didn't want me to be alone after she left and you know how convincing she can be. Listen, if I've learned anything in this program. It's how to take direction, especially from Mary Helen."

We had talked several times after that and the last time I got to see Danny was at Gay's memorial. When we hugged good-bye, I told him, "And I don't forget I'm still an asshole." It embarrassed him a bit, but before he could say anything else, I Said, "No Danny, it's truly an honor."

GiGi B

I got sober thirty-four years ago at the World AA Convention in New Orleans. I went with my mom. I knew I was an alcoholic, I just hadn't faced the facts. I ended up at the AA Convention and I was confronted by a man. He said, "Are you an alcoholic?" I knew I was. I didn't know what to say. He said, "Let me ask you this. Is your life unmanageable?"

I couldn't think of one area of my life that was manageable in my whole entire life. I came back from New Orleans to Palm Springs and started going to meetings. I had gone to New Orleans with my mom. When we drove back there was a girl in our park. She said, "GiGi you'll never guess what happened. While you were gone the girls in our park went out for the Fourth of July and they got in a horrible accident. One of them is dead and the other one is in jail for manslaughter."

All of a sudden I knew it wasn't going to be hard to tell them I'd quit drinking. After that I started going to meetings from Palm Springs to Palm Desert and also Indio at the ABC Club. That's where I did meet Danny and Helen and loved them immediately. I could see it was one home that we met at and there were sofas along the walls. People from the railroad tracks and people from the street were sitting along the floor and sofas. There was a little lectern.

Everyone could recognize the disease in everyone else. It was a real comfortable place to be. People would be in the kitchen cooking and bringing out birthday cakes, food and whatnot. I met Danny and Helen and sometimes we would go to Denny's and have coffee. We'd sit around and laugh and talk about our experiences drinking and share our experience and hope with each other. From one alcoholic to another. That's the common bond. The thread that runs through all of us. That knowing of one alcoholic to another.

They would bring the guys and women from the ABC Club to Fellowship Hall. We just all bonded and got to know each other.

Danny and Helen always took everyone in even if they had to sleep on the floor. Everyone was welcome and that was what I loved about Danny and Helen so much. They had a heart and love for the alcoholic. Eventually I started going to meetings, the women's meetings, and getting to know everybody. There were meetings at Helen's house.

I would go three times a week to karate on Miles Street, and then I would go to Helen's house with bruises and she would get out the ice packs. It was the camaraderie, and the real love for each other. I grew to love Danny and Helen like they were second parents. Along the way I met many fabulous people through them. We all rallied around each other and lifted each other up.

We had meetings, we had conventions, and we all got to go whether we could afford it or not. At the conventions I met very special people.

As time went on the ABC Club was growing. I just happened to be looking for employment at the time, and I ran into Gay Henchey. She was working at Leather Plus at the time and she mentioned there was an opening. That Diana W was running the store and she said to call Diana. I called her. She said, "Absolutely, come on down." I went to the store. I asked her if I needed to fill out an application. She said, "No, your starting."

So away I went. We were on the corner of Towne and Miles a couple of years. Then we ended up moving around the corner to Oasis. I worked there for quite a few years. The store grew. The clientele grew. Helen was coming down all the time, and it was really fun. Helen would come down, and Sunny would come down and decorate the store. It gave us more time to spend with each other, and put the store together. It was such a beautiful place. So many pieces were donated from the Vintage Country Club. It was like little girls playing in the store. It was so fun, and us making everything look beautiful. People from all over would come in because we had pieces and parts from all over the world. They would come in and purchase pieces. They didn't even want to tell their friends. They kept us to their selves because we had such beautiful stuff.

We had a lot of repeat customers. That was Helen's pride and joy. Her and Sunny would come down, volunteer, and make everything look fabulous. We all played together and helped. It was an exciting time. Danny and Bill would come over about lunch time and take Helen and Sunny to lunch. Sometimes them and all of us would go out together. Then we'd come back and start out together. Danny always looked forward to coming to the store to see how things had progressed and what fabulous pieces and parts we had got. It was always a spirit of camaraderie and love. There was lots of joy and happiness in the store.

Doing something to help the ABC Club. The money went to the ABC Club. That is where our hearts were. Danny and Helen's hearts were there. Everybody that worked there pulled together and we did the best we could for the ABC Club. The ABC Club was where we started out. That's where people came and got healed and loved, and given a new start in life. Leather Plus was our common bond to help one another, to help the next person that came along.

That's really what the whole program is about. One alcoholic helping another. I can truly say from the bottom of my heart there was never a day that Danny and Helen didn't hold their hands out and welcome people in. They gave second chances, and third chances for people that couldn't make it the first, or second time. They were always there whether they had packed their shit, or not. They were always welcomed back. I hope you get to know Danny and Helen the way we did, because they were truly angels on the planet and I loved them dearly.

Juan G

I'm forty-five years old. In September 27, 2005 I was arrested for the last time. Thanks be to God. After a few months of serving in county jail I was offered a program at the ABC Club, December 8, 2005, where I gained the best foundation in recovery I would have ever imagined. I always thought I would get recovery at Betty Ford, or Loma Linda Behavioral, or Malibu Passages. One of these fancy dancy places. Who would have known right at the battle front of addiction there on Palm Street and Indio Boulevard at the ABC Club.

I had heard good things about it, but I always thought I would need to do a geographical change. In some cases recovering alcoholic and drug addicts do need to make that change. But for myself I felt it would be hard for me to gain recovery when I might know persons that I might have drank with and associated with. That wasn't the case. Being here locally, it gave me a better understanding of recovery so I was extremely grateful, because even to this day I attend meetings at the ABC Club. I've branched out also at other fellowship meetings NA, or AA. I was extremely grateful when I was offered the program.

I had a violent past. I don't minimize my behavior anymore. There was a time I minimized it, but through the program I learned not to minimize it. I was glad I met Danny Leahy, Helen, and Bill W and many others.

How I met Danny Leahy was by chance. My wife knew that she wanted to help me still and somehow, through the guidance of God met others, and from there got Danny Leahy to go on my court date December 8, 2005. So I didn't have to wait long when I was offered recovery in lieu of state prison time. The judge said, "We will need to find a place that is willing to take you. They'll need to know your background, and be somebody that's willing to take you."

One thirty, or two o'clock in the afternoon and Danny's five foot plus stature stood up and said, "I'll take him your honor." That's the first time I ever met him. I had heard his name, but never met him. He stood up in the middle of court and stopped the proceedings.

The judge had to tell him, and knew him by name, "Okay Danny I got you. Okay sit down now for a minute."

In county jail many people had started to read the Bible. St. Paul and whatnot. They talked about Danny Leahy as if he was one of the prophets in the Bible, because he was there saving so many lives. He did so much for people. I said God just let me have the ability to meet someone like himself that will go to bat for me, and stick out their neck for me. So he did.

That's the first time I'd met Danny and thus went to meetings at the club. So I am extremely grateful. Then after that I met Helen, his wife, at a meeting I attended called CODA. Helen had that meeting on a Wednesday with a few others so I got to interact also with her. It was such a blessing to get such essential tools. Essential tools, life skills from her also, and many others.

After a few months of being there at the ABC Club the good news and the bad news. One door closes and another one opens. I had been a postal employee for seventeen years at a main office in Redlands. As a direct result of my alcohol and drug use I lost my job, or gave my job away. I gave it away by the bad choices I made. I was given the opportunity to work at a place called Leather Plus that many are familiar with. It since has closed. It was great because I needed that. In a job environment that would protect myself. Working in recovery with the proceedings going to the ABC Club gave me a better recovery. It wasn't the money, but it gave me the opportunity to be there. I needed to get a job and I was glad they made the offer.

I'm glad now. As of this day I've been gainfully employed by Riverside County. I never thought I would be able to get a civil service job. I've been with the County of Riverside for the last four years.

I was in the club thirteen months. I was sentenced there for one year. I waited another month before I left. I wanted to make sure everything was good, and it was. I didn't want to be in a hurry to leave and I'm glad they let me stay another month. Even after that I attended so many meetings there. I couldn't get enough recovery. It was a blessing. I got to meet with Danny, not only in meetings, but he always made himself available and that was a good thing. I heard it how I needed to hear it from him and Helen. Danny had a way with words. He didn't beat around the bush. He was direct. He had experience too. He knew that people like myself had a tendency to want to manipulate the system.

He said right away, from the get go, "What we're going to do here is save lives, and if you want to save your life this is what you need to do." I took direction. My Higher Power, my God gave me the willingness to take direction, and surrender which I do daily.

Danny wasn't tall, he wasn't big in stature, but he commanded respect. So when he came around, even though I wasn't doing anything wrong, I felt like I was. I always felt like I should be doing something more.

They had the world famous PYSM that people used to quiver in their seats. He kind of did an inventory of person, or persons there. The audience were all there and if you're not doing your program, or neglected to do your chores, he said, "Go upstairs and pack your shit." I didn't look forward to that meeting even though I was doing my program and doing what I could. That has been, to me personally, one of the biggest catalysts to move me forward. I did have a tendency, and I have a tendency to, in my drug use, manipulate people. In my alcoholism I would do what I needed to do to continue my behavior. But you couldn't do that with him, and others, like Bill. And I associated with them. You could talk to them twenty minutes to give them a two second excuse. It was, "Get to the point. Why ain't you doing this? Why aren't you paying this?" I'm glad they were how they were. There was no room for short cuts, and I'm grateful.

The ABC Club being close to home, and being close to my family gave them the opportunity to go to meetings. I didn't meet a lot of people that I would have drank with. Maybe now I have, but also I had the blinders on. I was extremely focused. I wasn't there to associate. I wasn't there to make friends. In the long run I did make many friends that I have kept as of today. I was there to gain a foundation like I was told by my sponsor, and I was told by my detox manager when I was there, Kenny Earhart, I'm glad I learned so much and have maintained some of those thoughts in my head that I heard while I was there.

Like Danny would say, "You won't get recovery through osmosis. You can come to meetings, hang out with sponsors, be around many alcoholics, but if your not doing the footwork you're not going to get clean and sober. You need to participate, you need to work the steps, you need to meet with sponsors, you need to go to meetings, you need to abstain from going to places that will give you triggers." All these things essentially I did know, but I always thought, well maybe there is a way I could continue this, but from the get go I knew that was not going to be possible even to this day. It's been my everyday thought in my life to continue to do what I am doing, to continue to do what I've learned. I know I won't get another chance, just like I've heard him say.

I'm extremely grateful that I was sent there. I would have never thought the ABC Club. Not that it was some dungeon place or any thing like that. I had thought how am I going to get recovery from my neighbor kind of thing. Where I drank around, hung out, on the street. That is the best location I would have ever thought for it to be. Right there on Indio Boulevard. I remember back in my drunken state driving through there. Taking a short cut through there.

God smiled upon me when he said, "This is where you are going to go." I had tried other places. My insurance sent me to Loma Linda Behavioral, Betty Ford, and I did try one, but I left. They held my hand in the mornings, and tucked me back into bed. Ten days later I'm ready to go. I think I'm cured. It's the opposite at the ABC Club. It's get up, you got commitments, you got to do this, you got to do that. That's what I feel like when I've got sponsees and I work with others. We need to be accountable. We need to have commitments in our recovery. This getting up at twelve in the afternoon doesn't work. This addiction is waiting just across the weekend, and we need to be working toward our recovery. I'm glad we have that at the ABC Club.

Charlie M

My first introduction to Danny was in '92. I went to the ABC Club because I didn't know what to do. People said I should go there. I was trying meetings and whatnot. I sat in the office and Danny came out and he talked to me. He could see through my BS. He said, "You still got a watch on your hand. Your not ready."

I thought, alright I'm out of here. So it was another four years and I got court ordered to the ABC Club, for a year, or a five year sentence. I thought I had another court date and I had some things I had to put off for awhile. I went to the court. I was going to say I was going to take my chances on the five years and not go to the ABC Club. I went to the court and there was no court. I wasn't on the docket, so I thought I'll just go to the ABC Club. I was very troubled, very troubled. I didn't think I could do it. I was court ordered for a year. I had a broken jaw. I was living on the streets.

Life was a mess. Stayed there in house nine months and went to sober living for six months. I went to school. I went to meetings. Made friends. I learned how to stay sober. I couldn't do it. I tried going to meetings for years. Would I get in trouble? I wasn't feeling well about drinking. But I never really had the desire to quit. Even when I went to the ABC Club I didn't have the desire to quit. I just wanted to get out of trouble. I learned in there that there is a way to stop drinking. There is another life.

Danny and Helen played a big part. My dad died in '94. I didn't know how to handle it emotionally, so it led to a lot of drug use, and I was drinking, and living on the streets. I just gave up and said, "I'm going to do what I want."

When I went into the ABC Club, Danny, I looked up to him almost as a second father figure, as a person to show me guidance. He showed me how to work the program. He called me on my BS. He let me know if I'm doing things right, or wrong. During the PYSM I was getting nervous, and there was nothing to get nervous about. He'd say, "If you're doing what you're supposed to be doing there's no reason to get nervous." I was doing what I was supposed to be doing plus a little extra. He didn't know about that. I was just messing with people and little stuff like that. You always get nervous for those. He definitely showed that there's a different way of life, but I couldn't stop drinking. I needed help.

I was scared of Helen. I think she saw through my BS more than Danny. She could call it a whole lot quicker. She didn't put up with any crap. Danny, if he liked you was a little lenient at times. I think Helen could see right through people. That kind of scared me. She kept me on my toes and helped me with the classes.

Some of the exiting classes: I went to the parenting classes, writing checks, and Bill did that one, and exit plans where Tim A was there. Helen would sit in on some of those. Then there was meditations. We went to a lot of meetings. Mechanic Tom would come in and sit around and share. I enjoyed my time there. It was actually easy living. While I was there I'd go do a little bit of work, do some chores. Get fed. Make friends. Go to meetings. It made getting sober fun. Enjoyable. Anything was better than what I was doing.

I stayed sober until '98-'99 and then I went back out. Decided I knew better. I found out quickly I didn't know better. I had nowhere to go. I could have kept going, but my head was crazy. The insanity. I think it was because I knew there was a way to change. I knew I could stop drinking. I just had to be willing to go do it. I knew there was another life and what I was doing it was not the right way to do it.

I went back into the club. I was there for six months. I stayed sober for quite a while after that. The second trip back into the club was an eye opener. It wasn't the same. As far as my sobriety. It was a little more serious, even though I didn't have a sentence. I didn't want to go do that again. I had met Kathy. I went in the club and a month later she went into the Ranch. Even though we were told don't do this, don't do that we found our ways and we did what we did.

I remember before I left Bill had taken me to court a few times, and Danny. Bill was going to court with me. It was between Kathy, with the District Attorney, and me. Finally I agreed to their terms. Whatever I would take classes and whatnot. Bill said, "You're good to go Charlie. You've fulfilled what ever you need to do, your terms and you're good to go."

In the PYSM I told Bill I was going to leave in a couple of weeks. Danny said, "You're going to go back to that same thing, with that same women."

I remember hearing that and going, "No, I'm not. You're going to be wrong this time." Luckily things worked out.

It is a great place. It opened my eyes and let me know there is another way of life. I tried AA six months, but I'd stay sober for two weeks. People would say, "Hey, keep coming back. Take a drink, but keep coming back." Okay, and I'd go drink and I'll keep going back and finally said this wasn't working. I got myself in some major trouble down the road, but I met a lot of people at the club.

I definitely miss Danny and Helen. They really saved my life, and the club and Bill and everybody that worked there.

I'm in between jobs right now. I'm collecting workers insurance. I had a good job working with solar. I've got a couple of jobs, one in Vegas. There's one in Blythe going up. I've been looking. I've had a few things come up.

Taryn I

I went to the club twice. The first time was in 1999. I ended up at the club because of drugs and alcohol. I came out here from the beach to the desert and I ended up at the ABC Club. The first time I was there almost two years. I relapsed after a couple of years. I went back in June 2002 and I was there for a year and a half that time.

I had been living on the streets for awhile and when I got to the club everybody was real friendly, and the staff was nice. Danny wasn't there for the first week that I was there, but when I did meet Danny I was kind of afraid at first, because I didn't know what to expect from him. But after while when I got to know him, he was loving, and kind, and generous, and willing to help anybody with their sobriety. He was very compassionate.

I loved Helen too. Helen was amazing. I was more definitely afraid of Helen, than I was Danny. I got to know her through the meetings. When I came back to the club in 2002 Helen was my sponsor. She was very blunt, and forward with me, with working the steps, she didn't hold anything back. She always told it like it was and really helped me along in my sobriety. She was willing to hold my hand through the whole process. She took me through my CODA steps which was a great thing to do.

Before I went to the club I didn't know how to handle any situation, or really live. When I got to the club it was all structured, and that was exactly what I needed. They taught me how to vacuum, to clean, and do all those daily things. I worked in the kitchen and I learned how to cook a little bit. They taught me to live life on my own so I would know what to do when I got my own place. I'm thankful still that the club was there, and that Danny and Helen were so willing to take anybody in, no matter what. When I went back to the club in 2002 I had no money. I didn't have anything and Danny took me in. He let me stay there. He told me I could stay for sixty days even though I didn't have a dime to my name. He told me I needed to follow his direction, and do everything my sponsor told me and not mess up, otherwise I had to leave. I ended up staying a year and a half.

I went through the club first, and detoxed, and then to the Doll House, and then to the transition house, and then after probably six months I made it over to sober living. The first time they didn't have sober living. I believe it was being built at the time. It was brand new. It's definitely different now than it was then. Danny didn't kick you out. After sixty days he let you stay and get situated, and get a job. Work a job.

Danny was so funny. I would like to go ride my skateboard around town. If I didn't have anybody with me, he would make me take Fred the dog. He made me take the dog with me when I'd ride my skateboard down to wherever, like Yellow Mart, and we would go down to Leather Plus. Wherever I wanted to go he would make the dog go with me. I guess so I wouldn't be alone. It was great, because I never felt alone, and I had to look after Fred, and keep out of trouble. I appreciated that.

I was managing a restaurant at one of the local hotels for about ten years. Recently I resigned from that job and now I'm going to COD (College of the Desert) to become a drug and alcohol counselor. I really want to be able to give back, like Danny and Helen gave to me. They really gave me my life back. It's just the way the whole program was there. It was very loving. I never, even growing up with my mom I never felt at home. There was always something missing. When I got to the club it felt like everything came together. Everything was brighter. I had people surround me that cared and loved me. The staff and Danny and Helen. They taught me how to be part of this world. They taught me how to be a better person, what I needed to do. The basics. I had no clue. Like showering every day. Getting up and going to a meeting. Taking time for myself by either taking a nap, or just relaxing. Cleaning. How to live life. I'm very grateful for them.

I really want to follow my dream of being a counselor in recovery, because I've seen a lot of things my friends have gone through programs the past couple of years. It seems to me it's like a business now. The money does matter. I just want to give back like they've given to me. They have been my inspiration about going back to school. I want to do my internship at ABC. I know it's changed, but it's still the club and I still want to give back. Danny and Helen put so much heart and love into that place. I want to be able to keep that going.

Jodi G

My introduction to Danny and Helen was through my mom and step dad in 1978. Madd Dog Daze committee meeting was at the original house. That is all there was in 1978, the rest was added on later. I was eighteen and just off the airplane from Washington State. My parents said that if I was to stay with them I had to attend AA meetings.

I wasn't convinced that I was alcoholic so I went out to do my research coming humbly back in April 2, 1979. Still eighteen and wild as could be. By 1982 I married and begin to have my family where my (at the time) husband entered ABC in 1985. This really threw me into activities at the ABC Club including a retreat for a week up in Idyllwild in July of 1985.

Sue Riley was the coordinator and we all had to attach a name in front of our name that best described us. Jolly Jodi became my name. Dastardly Dave was my husband's name. We broke up into groups and had little skits and sang songs, but changed the lyrics to fit our sobriety. Danny and Helen taught us to enjoy ourselves, that we were never too old, or too young to have fun in sobriety.

My first born was two and my daughter was one month old. Now this is funny. I was breast feeding and beings my daughter was not with me I had to continue pumping and put all the milk in little baggies. Danny and Helen allowed me to keep my breast milk stored in the freezer while at the cabin.

I think Sunny W is the only one who might have been there that's still around.

Charlie B

I came down in 1988 to go to school. Vince L, who was my roommate at the time came down with me to go to school. We had gone to a meeting, and Vince had met this guy. The guy said, "Come on. I'll take you to a place you will find interesting." Over we went.

It was the first time that I met Danny. I didn't meet Helen for a little while after that. I met a girl in the San Fernando Valley four years prior to 1988. We dated for awhile. Little bit of separation in our age. I came to find out Helen was her cousin. It was kind of a shock. I'd gone back up to the San Fernando Valley weekends. Breaking the connection back there was hard. I'd swing by this girl's house, her mother's house, to see how everybody was. It was that conversation that she said her cousin, Mary Helen and her husband Daniel lived down in the desert. The next time I saw her she told me that her cousin and her cousin's husband have a recovery home in Indio. I said, "The ABC Club?"

She said, "Yes."

I said, "Oh my God that's my sponsor." So it was a little bit of a tie-in that we had right there before we even met. Through the years we found out other things we had in common.

I was less than two years sober and I called up my then present sponsor who had told me when I left Los Angeles to find somebody down here that I could ask to be my sponsor. I told him in my little arrogant way that if I had to move to east BF Egypt you are still going to be my sponsor. After I'd met Danny and I'd finally turned two. I wrote a letter to my first sponsor and thanked him for being there and taking me through the steps. For being there when I was whining about relationships and everything else. I found somebody I could ask.

We had a sponsor, sponsorship friendship for twenty-one and a half years before Helen and he moved to Oregon. I had a pretty good relationship with Helen because of that connection. We used to laugh about it.

The girl came down here. Her parents called me. She had problems with drugs and alcohol. They put her into the Ranch. I didn't think about asking the ABC. She got booted out of there for fraternizing.

One of the guys that worked there drove her to the ABC and dropped her off there. She was in ABC for two, or three months.

Danny wanted me to work at the ABC Club. He wanted me to get involved in areas where Gary P eventually got involved in. I had one little time in my sobriety where I worked at Michael's House. I worked there for a week. I said no this just ain't doing it. I never felt comfortable working at a recovery place. Danny had asked me a couple of times that first year that he sponsored me. I know he forgot my name. He kept calling me his favorite day word. Every time he seen me he'd say, "Hi. How you doing? You sponsoring somebody?"

"Don't they have to ask me Danny?"

"You come over to the ABC Club."

I went over after a meeting. I walked in to his office. He said, "Come with me." I walked out into the room and that was when we still had couches down stairs. He pointed to three different guys and said, "You, you, and you come here." They all walked over and he said, "Meet your new sponsor," turned around and walked out. I had three resentments looking at me. To my knowledge they all went back out, but I heard one came back and stayed sober. That happened with the first five, or nine people I sponsored.

I went to Danny and said, "Danny, no ones staying sober, just like Bill Wilson and Lois."

Danny said, "Well, you are stupid." I thought, oh yeah I am aren't I, how about that. It was an eye opening thing.

Danny was never soft with me. I was a little over two years sober when I asked him to sponsor me. Thirteen years later my sister lived in Northern California. My sister called me at three o'clock in the morning and said, "Dads got an aneurism on his heart." I told Kay I got to go up, so I got up and left about four o'clock in the morning. It was about an eleven hour drive. We tried everything, different doctors and stuff. Finally we took him to Enloe. It's a big trauma hospital in Chico California. They happened to have a vascular surgeon on call at the ER. He took one look at dad and said to get him in the operating room right now.

I called Danny. I didn't know what to do. Every time we had a prior conversation he would never say, I love you Charlie, unless I said it first.

I'd say, "Love you Danny," and he would say, "I love you too Charlie." Then we would go about our way. We were on the phone five, or ten minutes and he said, "It's going to be alright Charlie because he is in God's Hands." Then he said, "I love you Charlie." 'Wow,' I thought. He hung up, and when I got back down to the valley I had all kinds of people at ABC coming up to me and saying, "Charlie, how's your dad?"

I thought, how the fuck do these people know about my dad? I asked one guy, "How did you know about my dad's stuff?"

He said, "Charlie, when you called it was right in the PYSM."

Danny had just stopped and took the phone call and talked to me. That was one of my real first examples of the program working. One alcoholic talking to another. He was a special individual. He was a good friend. My dad passed back in '07, and my mom had passed and I had went through some real tough grief with my mom. When my dad passed Danny came over and said, "Come on, get in the car." I was in my shorts and a tee shirt. He at least had a nice shirt on and chinos.

I said, "Where are we going?"

He said, "Well this friend passed and they are having a memorial for him at Fellowship Hall."

"But Danny I look like."

"Get in the car."

So I got in the car and went over to where it was being held. I sat way in the back and I listened to all the eulogies about this guy. I knew him and had said hi to him a few times. I didn't know him as a friend. His son got up and talked about his dad. Oh my God it hit me right between the eyes, because it was him and his dad, and me and my dad who had just passed two months prior to that. I walked through my grief that day. I was okay. I grieved my mom for over a year and a half, painfully. I grieved my dad two months. Because Danny said, get in the car.

I walked through the reception line and thanked the son. I told him he had helped me tremendously. That I didn't know him, but his father a little bit. It was all about listening to my sponsor when he told me to do something.

We had gone down to San Felipe Men's Retreat a couple of times. I was one of the first ones that got involved with that. Danny pretty much stayed with the rest of the guys. They had a pretty good retreat. I went to some of them, and then quit going.

I would go talk to him in his office. You know how everybody would pile into his office. They hadn't gone over to the Leahy Building yet. One day I was in the office and Helen was at her desk. Three, or four of us were all in there talking. Danny was in his office and he comes out. He and Helen got into it. I mean it was a donnybrook like you wouldn't believe. Everybody starts leaving the office like rats leaving a ship. They were yelling at each other. He looked at me and said, "Get out of here."

I said, "No, you are going to make an ass out of yourself and I'm going to stay and watch." He turned back to Helen and they started going into it again.

He looked at me again and said, "Get out of here."

I said, "No." Eventually I left.

I was there the next day and he comes out of his office and says, "Helen would you come in here?" They closed his office door and I could hear laughing and giggling going on.

I need to know how to do that. When I blow up like that I need to know how to be able to talk to my spouse. Kay and I had just got together. We were living with each other. Every time I got into a donnybrook like that with a wife, or girlfriend I would put on my shoes, I'm out of here, and take off.

Helen was a special person. I could sit down and talk to Helen. There were times I'd call over there and Danny wouldn't be around. I almost had two sponsors when Danny was my sponsor. When they were in the process of moving to Oregon I went over to see Danny and he wasn't there. Helen said to me, "When I first heard I had cancer it was a shock, but you know, after the initial shock I was okay with it. I was ready to move on. I knew Danny would absolutely come apart." She went through three and a half years of chemotherapy. And Danny did when she passed. He loved her so much.

I had just met Billy and I asked her how old she was. She said twenty. I said okay and she asked me if I ever lived in Palm Desert with a women and a black guy. I told her yes and she said that was her birth mother. Danny drove in just when I was leaving and he said, "You stay away from my granddaughter."

"What the hell are you talking about?" Well Renee, Helen's daughter, had married Billie's father, and Renee adopted Billie. I came back from working at the Hyatt one day. Vince and I had talked about it. That if anybody needed a place to go we could help out. Vince invited one girl. She wasn't going to meetings, she wasn't looking for a job, she wasn't looking for a place to stay. After two weeks I told Vince that he had to tell her to leave. You asked her now you have to tell her to leave. He did. Within two days she was going to meetings, and she found a place to stay and she found a job. We were enabling more than we were helping. I came home one day and the couch was pulled into a bed, and the bed was vibrating. It was a girl detoxing. She was shaking so bad. I looked at Vince and he said somebody dropped her off, and had heard we could help her. She stayed sober. Vince went out. I found out that when we came down here he was only sober almost six months, and I thought he had seven years. I was one and a half years sober when we came down here and I was crazy as a loon.

I moved down here and finished up school that I started in 1962 and I graduated in 1990. Twenty years to get a two year degree. Danny was my sponsor and I met Helen and got involved with the ABC Club. Eventually met my wife at COD (College of the Desert) and my life changed.

Michelle R

How I got to the ABC Club? I'd been on methadone for eleven years. Was doing a lot of heroin at the time. My kids were sick of it so they told me there's a party in the desert and they dropped me off at David Johnson's house and left me there. I had an ultimatum to either get clean, or go live on the street.

I came down here and got on the methadone treatment and started detoxing. I had to get to thirty five milligrams because I was at one hundred ten. There was a gentleman that worked at the methadone clinic that helped me get into American Hospital. I got into the American Hospital. At the time I was staying with David Johnson, and Joe Nielson who worked at the club. After seventeen days at the American Hospital the deal was that Danny and Helen said I could come to the club. But I had to go straight from the hospital to ABC.

During the time I was detoxing I was hanging around and going to meetings at ABC and I was not especially happy about it. I didn't really care for those meetings. I happened to be there during Sharon Koski's group. She did not want to let me in there because I was late. I asked Helen if I could stay there and she said, "Sure. but we don't have any beds right now, so you may have to sleep on the floor, or on the couch." That was fine, I was grateful to do it. I stayed on the couch probably three weeks, because there wasn't any beds. I finally moved upstairs to the Doll House. I started liking it. When I look back on it, it was one of the happiest times of my life.

It was fun. There were lots of characters to meet. I stayed ninety days. Sterling (son) ran away and I had a safe place to go, so I just kept going to meetings there. I don't think I would have ever got sober if it hadn't been for that place. It gave me a new lease on life being there. I would go back and hang out and sponsor people and see Danny and Helen. I got Helen as my sponsor. It was a couple of years. I was cleaning houses with KK and Terse was the secretary. It just so happened that she quit, or something. I called Helen and asked for the job. I got it. God those were wonderful times. That's when I got to know Danny and Helen and work really closely with them.

I got to know Danny and listened to his story. It always amazed me that once I got to know him so well how, makes me cry, he got sober. Talk about the odds being against him.

Danny stories just blow me away. It was when he would get that really crappy coffee. It was awful and nobody could stand to drink it. My mom had a shop next to Folgers. So when I would go up there I would bring letters to try to get them to donate coffee. One day this guy shows up from Folgers coffee and he said, "You know we donate to so many people we can't donate, but we can give you a real good deal on."

Danny was like, "You know we really don't have any money." So we were all dejected and defeated because they couldn't donate us any coffee. About ten minutes later this little old man came running in the front door.

"Hey, do you guys need any coffee? Because I've got a truck load of it out there I need to get rid of." He just gave us all this coffee. It was regular coffee. I couldn't believe it, here was all this coffee. We had just been dejected because we didn't have any coffee. That is when I thought, God really does take care of this place. Those were happy times for me. Working with Danny and Helen. They were both such characters.

I worked there twelve years. It was fun. Sometimes it was difficult. Danny and I argued a lot. I really loved him. We all have character defects, but I think I loved every one of them. He walked like he talked. You couldn't really put anything by him. He'd heard it and seen it all. I liked being around him. I really never had a male figure in my life. Danny and Bill kind of fit the mold. I could go to them with anything. They were fun times. Helen was a character too. What I liked about Helen is she never told you whether you were doing right or wrong. She would ask, "Well, what do you think? How do you feel about that?" She never belittled you. She was kind and loving.

I hadn't been working for a while. I had just broken my leg. Leather Plus needed an office manager so I got the job. I worked there for about a year. I liked it because I got to see Helen and Danny. We'd go to lunch. It was hard to watch her, because some days when she'd come in and she had taken steroids, it wasn't good to see.

I think about all the people in my life and those two made more of an impact then even my family. Even though I relapsed and had a hard time, there's not a day that goes by that I don't think of them.

When Danny got really sick. It might have been Dawn who called me and told me he wasn't doing well. He wasn't getting up out of bed. He wouldn't go out. So one day I was in the neighborhood and I thought, well I'm going to stop and see what's going on. I went over there and it was two o'clock in the afternoon. He was laying in bed. I went in and crawled in bed with him, and sat there and talked to him. Got him up. He needed aspirin at Walgreen's to just get him out. Then I would go by a couple times a week. Sometimes we didn't go out of the house. Sometimes we did. I thought maybe if he sees Bill and Ralph, some people. I got there and he didn't want to go.

All excuses, so I told him, "Look, if you don't feel good I'll bring you back." He ended up having a good time. I would do that a couple times a week. At that time he needed to have someone come over a couple times a week to bathe him. He wasn't in good enough shape to get in the bath, or the shower by himself. I wasn't capable of doing it. I would go over and clean up his bedroom. Change his bed. We'd take him to lunch I'd get a couple of girls. He liked that.

When you did take him out you had to take enough oxygen tanks, and that the cords were not kinked, and that the oxygen tanks were full. You had to be on a time limit because he could only be out so long. One girl took him out at nine and didn't bring him back until midnight. That is when Dawn (stepdaughter) found him on the toilet and they had to call the paramedics. He had run out of oxygen. He went in the hospital and they had to do life support, and put tubes in him. A couple of days later they took the tubes out. There was nobody there for that. I told him he would get better. A few days later they took him to the convalescent hospital. I would go at lunch and dinner and cut up his food, and feed him.

It was the calm before the storm. What worried me is I didn't think when he was home that his nutrition was being monitored. I'd go over there and he would be eating a bowl of Cheerios. Danny was not good about his eating habits; he was terrible. I'm sure he had Medicare. I kept telling Dawn and her husband, Mondo, there needed to be someone coming in a couple times a week. To bathe him, clean him up. Make sure he has decent meals.

I don't think you can go anywhere and not run into someone who knows Danny and Helen. I believe in my heart they made sobriety the cool thing. I don't know if the ABC Club hadn't been, that there would be 'The Sober Capital of the World.' I feel they put it on the map. All their years of hard work.

Lisa E

I went to the club May 29, 2001. Danny had let me come back after a few times of being there. I was homeless. I had burned about every single bridge. My mother didn't want to help me out anymore. There was nobody left to burn anymore. The only place that would take me was the ABC Club. Danny Leahy let me back in after knowing I was a mess up. I was a mess. They had to send me to the mental hospital. After being there for a few days they realized I had speed induced psychosis. I was on anti-psyche medication for about thirty days. Then Danny said I didn't have to take them anymore. They were making me too lethargic.

While I was there at the ABC Club I learned how to do everything. I didn't know how to do anything before I came to the ABC Club. It wasn't even about staying sober. They taught me to set weekly goals and how to accomplish those. To have a laundry day, to set aside time for cleaning. To make those goals, and carry them out through the week.

Helen Leahy had a lot of groups on just being a women. A 'Women Who Love too Much' meeting. A relationships in general meeting. Not just a relationship with men, but a relationship with anybody, as a women. Learning how to deal with those kinds of feelings. How to have proper relationships. How to set boundaries with people. I still hear Danny and Helen talking to me. When I'm in trouble, or in times of need, I can hear them. I can hear what Helen would say to me.

Being at the ABC Club, the night time was usually a hard time for me. That is when I would get antsy. There wasn't anything going on after the meeting, and I was still amped up with a lot of energy. Danny would still be there after the meetings. After everything was done. He would have a mandatory walk. I never understood what those walks were about and I never wanted to do them. Looking back on everything, those walks are probably what kept me there. After the walk I would just be tired and I would go to sleep. Those walks got all of that antsy energy out. It was a time to think and reflect, and do something active at night.

The PYSM every Tuesday night and I was on every single list. I was always in trouble. They had meetings about me every week on whether, or not I should be allowed to stay there at the ABC Club. Helen Leahy, I find out years later, was the reason I got to stay at the ABC Club. She would say, "Give her one more day. Let her stay just one more day." She would say that at every meeting they had about me. I was really grateful.

Because of that I was given the opportunity to go back to school, and get my life together. No longer in that meth induced psychosis. It kind of went away after a few months. I slowly started landing back into reality. I got a job, started working, started paying rent, started going to school, and started getting simulated back into society.

It's been twelve years later, almost thirteen years. I'm a nurse. I worked as a nurse. I got my bachelor's degree. I have been able to help a lot of women because of them and my own experiences. I will always treasure my memories that I have of them. I know I wouldn't have stood a chance anywhere else.

I was supposed to go into a mental hospital. They understood people at the lowest parts of their lives. They understood a person in need. What I always remember about Helen is there was many people with a lot of money, and a lot of prestige that Helen was associated with, and who I always saw Helen with was the sickest people. The sickies. Those were her closest people around her. Those were her people. She had a tremendous amount of love for people that were in need, and that needed help with alcoholism.

I have a nine year old son and I had him sober. I had a slip six months ago. I drank again. For the most part my son never saw me drink until just recently. As an excuse to keep on drinking I thought people with twelve years don't ever lose sobriety and then get it back ever again. I really thought that, and it was going to keep me out there even longer. I remember reading in the back of the AA Big Book, the personal stories. The only time I read the personal stories was with Helen at her book studies. She shared that she had been sober for a while, and picked up a drink, and stayed sober after that. She went on to help thousands of women. So she has been my ray of light. It hit me that, okay, if Helen could drink again and then stay sober; I know I can stay sober.

Tony S

I was writing Danny to get on the waiting list while sitting up in jail. My mom and my brother bailed me out, and my sister-in-law Maria was bringing me to meetings. But I was still smoking a little pot here and there. We came in on a Monday night meeting when they were still smoking off of the dining area. I heard Danny get up and say, "KISS. Keep it Simple Stupid."

I went home and told my mom, at the meeting was Foster Brookes. Remember the guy that played as the drunk on the Flip Wilson's show? That's who I thought Danny was. Then my sister-in-law told me that was Danny, that wasn't no Foster Brookes. I came to a chip meeting that Tuesday night. Stewart worked there and he told me to come back the next morning and talk to Danny.

It was a Wednesday November 30th. I came in the next morning and went to a meeting. Danny came to the meeting. The residents were there standing in the hallway; and I was standing in the hallway. He beckoned to me to come into his office and asked me what did I want. I told him I didn't know how to live. He called me an asshole. This old man don't even know me, damn, how dare him. He said, "I called you an asshole because you're just like me." That was the first time anyone ever told me the truth.

I said, "Well, I don't know how to live."

"I'll give you until 5:30 this afternoon, If you're not back here then we'll give the bed to somebody else."

I remember going home and telling my mom. "I'm going out for recovery. Give me a hundred dollars, cause I want to go get high before I go in." I didn't know that the whole time she was going to AlAnon.

First thing that come out of her mouth was, "I'll take you." So I went and got my hygiene's and everything and pulled up in the parking lot at quarter till five. She kicked me out and that's when my recovery started. My clean date is December 1, 1994.

I had a three year joint suspension over my head. A year, I was sentenced to the ABC Club. After my year was up I moved over to sober living. Me and Willie went to court with Danny, and Jerry Shuford was our little Eskimo. We each got our sentence expunged. While I was there Judge Sheldon told me it looked like good recovery and I could go home, and don't break no law, because I was still on felony probation. I looked at him and said, "I'm afraid to go home. I want to go to sober living." So he asked Danny, did he have a spot for me in sober living?

Danny said, "Yes." I could move across the street to the old motel. Before they burned it down.

I was twenty-two months clean and sober and Danny couldn't make it to the Men's Retreat up in San Pablo. He asked who the oldest one here is, and I was the oldest one in recovery at that time. Me and his grandson, Sean, went to the spiritual retreat with all the old timers. I think that's when my recovery really kicked up and I wanted to do this deal. So I come back and a week later Danny asked me how would I like to work for him? I said no. So I started training out for detox. I stayed there as the detox manager for four years and eight months.

Then I went to Betty Ford. I had learned so much from Danny and Helen. The thing that stuck to me the most about Helen was she always said, "You can't think your way into good living, you got to live your way into good thinking." That always stuck with me.

My brother-in-law had kicked out the back door of my daughter's mom's apartment and stole all the toys and went and pawned them for drugs and alcohol. I was so pissed and I went to Helen's Tuesday Relapse Meeting. She asked me what was wrong. I said nothing, I'm just going to kill this SOB.

She told me, "Tony it's not like you'd ever stole nothing from anybody." That always stuck with me. How can I get angry at something I used to do myself when I was out there. It was like a little growing experience that they gave me along the way.

When I went to Betty Ford I got caught up with one of the girls that came from prison, and the rumor was that I was screwing every female there, and screwing females in detox. It wasn't so. One wound up pregnant with my son, but she wasn't even staying there at the club. She had her own apartment. Rumors was rumors and the good thing about it was it was down the road three years ago. We were going to Wednesday's meeting and my friend Andy got up there and shared. Then Danny got there and shared. I was able to get up to the podium and identify and tell Danny I didn't understand then, what he was telling me, but I understand now, that I was sleeping with a cripple. I really didn't understand it wasn't no code of ethics. I was at a place that I didn't know right from wrong. I was going to put justification, page sixty-nine, I'm not the arbitrator of anybody's sexual conduct. I was able to get up there and ask him for forgiveness. That I didn't know then, but I know now that it was really inappropriate. Something I had to learn along the way.

I admire him and Helen for being there for us. I'm working at Michael's House now. I did come back and work at ABC for a while. Danny told me as alumnus we shouldn't shy away from meetings just because of what happened to him, and Helen. We need to be there for the newcomers. That's what it's all about, the newcomers. He kept coming around and going to meetings even though he got railroaded. Danny said, "Don't never give up and stop going to meetings. Be there for the newcomers." That's the reason I go there, to let them know what was taught to me when I came through treatment there. I've got an awesome foundation now.

When Danny got sick, me and Danny Jr went up there and Danny was worried that they were trying to push him off to a senior citizen's home. He asked me what I was doing and I told him I was working over at Michael's House. He told me I needed to get certified, and I needed to go back to school, and get some initials behind my name. I took that to heart and I'm signing up for the RAS Program. That's an addiction specialist. It's on line at the Brendan Institute. I've already registered and everything.

I had open heart surgery Friday the 13th in December. What had happened my anesthesiologist told me to count from ten backwards. I was praying to my God. When I came to they had me strapped down, I seen this light I heard God's voice that he did a divine intervention. The devil was trying to take me, but he told the devil, no I'm not through with him yet. I have some more work for his butt to do. I love taking my recovery to another level. I really appreciate being clean and sober.

I'm glad I come through the club. I've gained experience, knowledge and understanding that I have today. I don't think I could have went anywhere else and still be sober right now. I had to go through the recovery center that was old fashioned. Danny was straight to the point. If you're not done, you're not done. I have so much gratitude and appreciation for what they gave me over the years.

Dale S

May 22nd 2009 I was in county jail for assault with a deadly weapon. In a blackout I stabbed my brother. The public defender came up and said, "You have a drinking problem, don't you?"

"Yeah," I said.

He said, "Well I could get you a year in a recovery home. If your willing to do everything they say."

So, I figured I was in prison once in Flagstaff Arizona, and I know the program. I told him, "Sure I'll go to the ABC Club."

When I came in Danny said, "You're up to something, aren't you?"

"Just trying to get out of jail."

He said, "Well if you do everything I say to do at the ABC Club you'll have more than just getting out of jail."

They sentenced me for a year at the ABC Club. I started doing what they said. Got a sponsor.

Two months into the ABC Club, my mom died. I was just going to do what they said for a year. That's what I was going to do. A year and then I could go do what I wanted to. But my mom died and I didn't have a couch to run back to. I talked to my sponsor and started doing the steps. I didn't have nowhere else to go. The club was my home. I stayed there for nine months.

I was the assistant detox manager toward the end of it. I met my wife, Terry. We just celebrated fourteen years sobriety. Danny and Helen, Ken and Mary, and everybody came to the wedding in tie dyed tee shirts. Sam and Charlie B.

My life kept on getting better and better. I met Sam and we started our business. My probation officer said, "I want you to go to three meetings a week." I was going to the club everyday and making five to ten meetings a week.

I said, "That's no problem."

I remember when Charlie said, "Well how long do you have to have this court card?"

I told him, "Hopefully the rest of my life Charlie." I like the people that come in with court cards. I tell them the story, and that this thing is going to save your life if you let it.

After Danny and Helen left the club I went back to work there for about a year and half. I'm grateful for the club. It showed me how to save my life. Danny and Helen taught me the steps and if you don't do the steps, you aren't going to figure it out.

Sam C

I came to the club in '96 from Riverside. My friend Randy used to live in Riverside. He was a drug counselor at the methadone clinic. He got a call from Riverside that Sam was dying. What happened was that I contracted a severe case of meningitis. He drove to Riverside and picked me up, took me to his house in La Quinta. I fell on the floor unconscious, peed all over myself and ended up in a coma for five days.

He knew Bea at the club. He said, "Look I've got this friend of mine who is dying. He needs to get in." Bea got the approval from Bill. Danny was on vacation. They got me in the club in '96. That was my first journey.

I met Danny. The meningitis gave me temporary retina damage. My eyes wouldn't focus. I was a hundred twelve pounds. Danny fattened me up and started teaching me the program. A little while later my brother died of this disease. I couldn't make it to the funeral because I didn't have a car. Danny said, "Look, if you don't go to the funeral now Sam, you'll be sorry later on." Danny drove me to LA to my brothers funeral, which was really good.

I started on my journey. I was in the club itself for seven months. Then I was nine months at sober living. I started saving my money. An apartment came up and I moved to my apartment.

A week before my five years I got loaded. I went back out. I stopped trusting God. Danny used to tell me all the time, "No matter what trust God." That was the main reason, from looking back at it, but what started it was a relationship. What you have got to understand is that I was living in abandoned buildings and on the streets. For at least ten years. When you are living in abandoned buildings, in the gutter, you're not practicing relationships. Then seven years in the penitentiary I tried not to practice too many relationships in there. It's pretty safe to say that the last time I kissed a girl candy bars cost a nickel.

So I got in this relationship. First one in twenty years. It started off real good and about a year later it ended badly. It was all because of me. I made decisions based on myself that later returned to hurt me. We got in an argument and I started ignoring her. I stopped trusting God, and when I seen her kissing someone else it drove me crazy. It got worse, and worse without God. I didn't do what Danny told me. I didn't get loaded to get loaded. I got out there to commit suicide. I bought three fifths of Irish whiskey, a couple grams of heroin, and planned to check out. I kept waking up. Finally I couldn't do it anymore and I took a razor knife to my neck. That didn't work. I had sixty-seven stainless steel staples.

I come back to the club and Danny's laughing at me. I go, "What are you laughing at, Danny?" Danny came up to me and put his arm around me.

"God said no, huh Sam?"

I said, "Yeah."

"Don't worry Sam, God told me no lots of times."

It was a learning experience for me. Danny told me I needed to learn from it. I've been in two more relationships since then, and they've ended badly, but I've trusted God this time. God has taken me by the hand and walked me through it. In February I'll have fourteen years.

I used to go to the club every day and hang out with Danny and Helen. When I was trying to come back I was really struggling and Helen told me, "Sam, what's happened, happened, and what are you going to do about it now?"

Danny kept telling me, "You just come by here every day and hang with us Sam." That really helped me a lot.

Now me and Dale are in business together. We've been in business about six years. Things are going really good. I've got a house up at Tela Verra. I got a little settlement. My dad. I hadn't had any contact with my Dad in ten years while I was out there. When I got sober, I started doing my steps and my sponsor, and Danny both said that I needed to contact my dad, which was really scary. I did that and now we have a wonderful relationship. His wife died. My dad was a heavy drinker, but not an alcoholic. He was a gambler. When his wife died the kids got a settlement. I didn't realize that my dad had spent my money gambling. But then he ended up stopping drinking and he sold his condo, and said, "Eight years ago, when Thelma died you were supposed to get a settlement. I have it now for you."

It shocked me, so I bought a house.

Nicole V

I got to ABC Club June 27, 2000. I didn't understand why I was drinking the way I was drinking. My sister was there for a week prior to me. I ended up asking my mom for help and she took me down there. I decided to stay for thirty days. First two weeks I was there I slept on the couch in the transition house. Everybody said they didn't have room for me, but just ask Helen, and they would hopefully try and would find a spot for me. I slept on the couch in the dead of summer. Lots of flies. They let me stay, on the couch.

Then I got a room in the Doll House for the last two weeks I was there. I had a thirty day commitment. I had to get back to work; so I got back. My boss allowed me to stay there for thirty days. I worked for a management company. I went out on my own. I do computers for a living. I went out on my own about nine and a half years ago. I wouldn't be there without sobriety. I know that for a fact. I wouldn't be there if I didn't have Danny and Helen who helped pave the way. If that place wasn't there I don't know. My sister went through there a couple times, so they knew our family. They did so much for our family.

My sister didn't get it a couple times, but she is finally on that road again. She's doing very well. We owe it all to Danny and Helen. I didn't interact too much with them. I remember PYSM. I was a good kid, I just stayed and did what I was supposed to do. Definitely asking Helen. I was scared of Helen, to walk into her office, and ask to stay, if they could find a spot for me. I just never been in a position like that before.

I didn't lose the house, I didn't lose the job, I didn't lose all that, but didn't understand why I was drinking the way I was drinking. Having my sister there probably helped pave that way. Knowing it was kind of a safe place. It was. I'm grateful for it. So grateful it was there. I did a commitment there for probably a year. I was torch lady in the Thursday Night Women's Candlelight Meeting. Margo was my sponsor at the time and that was my commitment. I did the candles. I used to see Danny and Helen from time to time. Helen would go to that Thursday meeting. She used to go to the Tuesday meeting too, Women Who

Love To Much. I remember going to that one. Lots of inspiration. I just loved them. Anytime, every year I take my cake I always bring up Danny and Helen, and the ABC Club and what it stood for. Grateful for it. I wouldn't be where I am today without it

Mary Ann & Patrick S

(Mary Ann) We met at the ABC Club. He stalked me. We waited.

He asked, "What step is she on? Has she finished her steps?" I kept seeing him at meetings. He'd be wherever I was. I think what happened is he asked me to the Halloween Dance, but we never ended up going to that dance. We did date. We asked permission. He went to Danny to get permission to date me. I went to Helen to get Helen's permission to date him, so we wouldn't be breaking the rules. And we asked our sponsors. Then we dated for a while.

Then he was sitting there and he said to me, "You know, I've got the white picket fence in my back pocket and I'm ready." I looked at him and said, "Are you talking to me? What are you talking about?"

(Patrick) When I asked Danny if I could take her on a date, Danny asked me if she had done her steps. I said, "Yes.

He said, "Okay you can date her, just don't go sucking face on my property now."

After we had dated for a while we moved out. We moved in with Greg S. He had a two bedroom apartment and we rented a room from him.

(Mary Ann) Then we were in the car and he said to me, "If I gave you a ring would you wear it?"

(Patrick) What I said was, "If I buy you an engagement ring would you wear it? If not I won't bother."

(Mary Ann) I looked at him shocked and thought, 'not one more time I'm getting married.' But it felt right because we were both in recovery on the same path. We were both serious about our recovery.

So we planned our wedding and what it was is that we were so, so poor. We both had jobs, but minimum wage. We sent flyers out at the meetings. Dino in the kitchen made chicken mole.

For the reception one of the residents bought the chicken. Danny Leahy bought our wedding cake with food stamps. He told me not to tell anybody because he would deny it. Another resident, John B was Patrick's best man.

(Mary Ann) Christine C was my maid of honor. The resident council bought the flowers for our wedding. They voted to buy flowers for our wedding.

The minister canceled and Levita the psychic took his place. Levita the psychic took the minister's place and married us. The new comers had to be there. They had to set up the chairs outside and it was June. Adam W was the deejay with a boom box. We had a wonderful time.

I had my son who was fifteen at the time, and he gave me away. Who's three years sober now, and engaged to be married himself. We got married on AA's Sixtieth Anniversary, June 10th 1995. We didn't even know It was Founder's day. We just knew when I got a year on June 7th. Three days after I got here.

We will be married twenty years in June. Something worked. He said I was stalking him. John B introduced us and he said, "You've got to meet this guy. He's just as smart aleck and arrogant as you."

When I saw him I said, "What, that guy's an asshole. Why would I talk to him?" He pulled out all the punches; he turned on all the charm. And he won.

Now we have our other son who turned eighteen in August. He's going to the community college here. He's working. Trying to grow up. We both have worked in the recovery business for fifteen years. He's the Danny Leahy here, with the beard. We've been in different places together. We worked at Betty Ford. We worked at ABC. We worked at NCS. Now we are at Orange County Recovery Services. Patrick is the service director. I'm the client coordinator. I take care of the appointments and Patrick is the Danny Leahy.

Danny Leahy

Excerpts from some of Danny's talks.

I like to say that I'm no authority on nothing, I don't claim to be. I didn't come in to win friends and influence people. I came in because alcohol was killing me, and it's important I remember that. I don't know about you, but I have a tendency to forget things and I never want to forget where I come from. It's easy to go back there. A lot of people do. I used to go back there all the time.

I'm no speaker. I stutter, my hair is falling out, I got diabetes, emphysema, bronchitis, and I got you, and I've never had it so good. People ask me all the time, "How you doing Danny?"

I don't know about you but I'm a liar, a cheat, and a thief. When I was new an old timer used to come in here. I used to hate him because he said the same thing all the time. He'd say fifty percent of the people in the room are going out again. Twenty-five percent of that fifty percent are going to die out there, and the other twenty-five percent are going to fall in; and fall out of here. I knew he was talking about me. There were six people in the room. What would you have thought?

The God who I hated and didn't understand changed all that. I had a sponsor tell me, fake it until you make it. That's what I had to do with the Higher Power. I didn't want to have anything to do with a Higher Power. As you might have guessed, I'm an Irish Catholic and I was raised by the nuns. They got a hold of me and it was instant war. Besides I was a left handed Irish Catholic. There aren't too many left handed Irish Catholics running around. Not if they went to the Catholic school I went to. There was probably ten of us in the room out of thirty kids. None of them changed.

I like to talk about in the beginning. I was told when I was a newcomer; you take all the Irish Catholics out of Alcoholics Anonymous, and the rest of you can meet in a phone booth. I thought that was pretty cool.

Then there was me. If I would have known then what I know now I would have surrendered. But being the alcoholic I was, I needed a drink. I wasn't getting one, so I wasn't giving up, and I got the shit beat out of me. If you think you're like me and can drink, go on out there. It gets worse, it don't get no better. I've been here a long time and I have never had anyone come back in here and tell me how wonderful it is out there. You have a progressive disease and it's going to get worse, and worse and worse.

When I put alcohol in my body, I act crazy. Without alcohol I'm sweet, warm and wonderful. Being crazy is not a problem. Acting crazy is.

I got mixed up in preschool. Because my mother she had to go to work and my grandmother wasn't able to take care of me all day. So they put me in Catholic pre-school, and the nuns got a hold of me. If there's any nuns in here this evening, I have forgiven you. I always like to say that, because I spoke one time in Apple Valley and there was four of them after the meeting that came up. I couldn't believe it. They wanted me to apologize. So I left Apple Valley with resentments.

I got taken out of that school and put in a school for retardation when I was about five, six, right around there. The reason they put me in there was I was having problems and I couldn't pass the grade. I kept staying behind, behind, and behind. I was put in the school for retardation and I knew something was wrong. I got put in with the brothers. I kept growing. One day I took the ruler away from the brother and beat him with it. That afternoon my folks were there getting me out. That was the end of my experience with the Catholic school.

My whole family is alcoholic/drug addicts. My father, he died at thirty, my mother took an overdose at fifty. My baby sister died from emphysema from smoking that non-habit forming marijuana for thirty years. I flew her down here about thirty years ago, and put her in the program and kept her in the program for thirty-five days. She had a brand new baby, and she was up north driving under the influence of alcohol, and rolled the car with three kids in it. I went screaming and hollering and I finally got her talked into coming down here. So we flew her down and put her in the program. I took a Fifth Step with her. I told her everything. She was a lot like me when she was a kid. Sniffing paint, and running around with older kids and getting in trouble. Driving my mother nuts. Her father, my stepfather died at fifty of alcoholism. His liver exploded.

When I was in San Francisco I spent ten years in-and-out of institutions. Started off with juvenile hall. I ain't proud of that, but that's what it took. I was hard headed. I was a non-conformist; I always had to say that. I'm a non-conformist. I don't conform to your rules. I always wanted to live by my rules. Got in a lot of trouble. Always got caught. But not for everything, if I would've got caught for everything I'd still be in there. God took care of me a lot.

I used to run around San Francisco with a 357 long nose magnum. It looked like a cane. I got drunk one night and sold it. Probably it was a good thing I did because I definitely, probably, was going to shoot somebody. I was running around with a lot of crazy people back then. I was probably the craziest one in the bunch. Right after that I got caught doing something else and went to jail again.

Compared at how I used to do, I'm doing great now. It got crazy here this afternoon. Both phones going at one time in my office. I didn't want to get a cell phone. I fought it for a long time. Everybody was getting cell phones. I don't want a cell phone. What would I want a cell phone for. Now I got one, and I know it was a mistake. Everybody's got that number now. Here I am.

I've been involved in this house for thirty-six years. I've been running the place for that long. I spent nine months in the house when someone else was running it. The guy that was running it was sponsoring me.

I put myself into a position. My sponsor said, "You don't mess with the girls in the program the first year." I wasn't messing with the girls in the program. I was messing with the girls out of the program. I damn near got drunk. Come real close to it. I was going to meetings and after the meetings we were going out to the Old Mill Inn in Indio. The Old Mill Inn burned down.

We went in there one night. This girl I was dating, she was a waitress, and her girlfriend, and her girlfriend's boyfriend. The three of them were drinking. We were sitting at the table and we ordered drinks. I asked for a coke and the waitress kind of gave me a funny look. After while the drinks were down and I drank all the coke. The girl I was with she went into the bathroom and the other couple was on the dance floor. Before she came out the waitress came over and asked, "Are you ready for another round?"

I knew it was my turn to buy so I said "Yeah, sure, give them the same and bring me a coke," and before I could get the word coke out, she laughed.

She asked, "You're not really going to have another coke?"

I said, "You're right. bring me a double shot of vodka." I was going to show her. Who did she think she was. Make me look bad like that. She walked back to get the drinks, the girl I was with came out of the ladies room. The other couple came off the floor and everybody wanted to leave, and we walked out. That might not impress you, but it impressed me. After I got out the door the compulsion to drink lifted and it ain't come back.

I do what I was told to do. I was told to stay involved. I went home that night and I called Fred, who was managing the house. I told him what happened. He said, "You're crazy, you better get down here." I was living in a motel with a bed and a kitchenette, TV and a bathroom in it. He said, "You're setting your self up." So I took his advice and I packed up my shoebox and moved down here.

I joined the union. I got a job. The guy I went to work for was a great big guy. He had a reputation of whipping convicts. He liked doing that. He asked me what I was in jail for, and I told him murder. Me and him became instantly good friends.

I was told by a sponsor to save some money. I was always sniveling about it, "I'm only making $1.65 a hour. When I was in San Francisco I was making union wages." I was very upset about that. My sponsor told me to quit my crying and go to work and do the best you can, and well, do something about it. So I started saving five bucks each week. After a year I came up with $300 to join the union, and I went down and I joined the union. Labor Union.

It didn't take long to get a job, and I got a job. We were working out of town and I kept a bed here at the ABC Club. For security reasons. It was called saving your ass. If anything happened out there I knew I could run back here. Back in those days shit was always happening. Excuse my language. If you notice when I cuss, I don't stutter. Not a bit. When I'm drinking I don't stutter either.

I started doing what I was told to do and my life got better. I walked about the first two and a half years when I was down here. I was a year sober when I hit Indio. I had a year sober in the institution. I should have had four years sober in there, but I couldn't stand that word Alcoholics Anonymous. I'm not that bad. I have all these other defects of character, but I ain't that bad.

My father was an alcoholic and everybody else in my family were. I was never going to be an alcoholic and I ended up worse than them. I always could identify as an addict also.

When I came to Indio, that was a dirty word. Nobody talked about drugs in Indio. I stayed here and I worked out. We had a lot of jobs out of town. We were building these pools. I found out later on that the pools were for contaminated material that they were making. They had to store it some place. So we were building pools all over the desert, and they were filling them up with that stuff. It kept me sober. I worked on a crew where everyone was drinking. When they made the run I would have a root beer. Then it gets started, them calling me the root beer kid. "Oh, get the kid a root beer."

My kid brother, they were my half-sister and half-brother. We had two different fathers. He died at forty. His liver exploded. He was in Vietnam and was decorated. He had a purple heart. I don't know what happened because I wasn't there, but I heard rumors that the whole company he was in was wiped out. He brought that back with him and he couldn't live with it. And he had it made. He was good looking, blond hair, blue eyes, six foot one, and over two hundred pounds. Real good looking kid. The alcohol just tore him up.

It was about sixty years ago. Can you believe that shit. Do I really look that old, for Christ's sakes. I can't believe it. My God, it seems like the other day I graduated from high school. Your sitting there thinking, well shit he couldn't read in the fourth grade. I couldn't read in the twelfth grade. They kind of just pushed me right through. Gave me a diploma and said, "You graduated." That's what they used to do. I don't know what they do now. I held that secret for a long time. I was a good worker so I got away with it. I drove a truck. Back then to get a chauffeur's license you didn't have to take a written test. You had to have a fifth of Scotch. You take that down to Motor Vehicles and give it to the supervisor and he writes you out a drivers license.

I read the paper all the time, and then I get an alcoholic in here once and awhile that can't read. They're lying out there. They're still lying. Everybody reads. That's what the president says.

I love the humor that I've found in Alcoholics Anonymous. Everybody was laughing when I got here I looked around and they were all laughing. What are they laughing about. There's nothing funny in here. This is the end of the road. This is the last house on the block. Where do you go from here? And it's been a journey. It's been a great journey.

When I got out of school I had a little sweetheart that said she was going to marry me. She was a hula dancer. She was on the Ted Mach Amateur Hour. That's how far back it was. If anybody can remember the Ted Mach Amateur Hour on TV and the old black and white screens. Her and her sister was on there and it's the most fascinating thing I've seen in my life. I took one look at her and said I want what she had, I'll tell you that. It was disastrous. I put that women through hell. I never intended to. But the alcoholism tore me every which way but loose. I was a cheater. I'd lie and I'd cheat.

I always had filet minion in the house, and I was always out looking for hamburger. I've got a thing about hamburger. I got to have one once and a while, I thought. I stopped that. Alcoholics Anonymous stopped that for me, God who I don't understand. My wife Helen, she is here to give me my cake tonight. I've been married to her for what's going to be thirty-five years. I don't know about you, but I know about me. We don't have problems getting women, we have problems keeping them. I'm sure there is one, or two of you in the room who know what I'm talking about. 'Cause I'd go to any length to get one. Then once I got one the alcohol became more important. Or that other stuff. I've been known to take that also, especially yours. And I haven't had to do that since I came in here.

Everybody I was running around with, the people would tell me; my sponsor would tell me, "One day at a time. You don't have to do that anymore if you don't want to." I believed them, and I still believe them. It ain't easy. Not every day is peaches and cream. There ain't no holidays every day. When it's good, it's good and when it ain't it passes. I can guarantee that. No matter how bad it is, if you don't drink, or take any of that other shit, it will pass. Because it did for me. And like it or not your just like me. Your one of God's kids. And I can say that with sincerity.

I never thought in a million years that I would ever communicate with God. I communicate with God all the time now.

I had a couple of children with my first wife. The last time I seen them my son was one and my daughter was three. I'm saying this because I know there's people in the room who've lost their kids. I didn't lose mine. I ran away from mine. They scared the shit right out of me. I couldn't handle them. I tried but I couldn't handle them. I put them on a shelf and told them, "Stay there, I'll be back." Fourteen years later, one Christmas day night we were going to Fellowship Hall. Connie was there, my mother. We were going out the door and the phone rang and I had a policy. I don't take collect calls, because of the house. For a while I took collect calls and I had phone bills you couldn't imagine. Helen was going to divorce me over it. That's how bad the phone bills were.

The operator got on the phone and said, "There's a collect call from Kathy."

I said, "Operator I don't take collect calls."

A voice came through the phone, "Dad it's me Kathy." It was like somebody knocking me down. I couldn't believe it, but I knew it was her. Last time I seen her she was three. She was always three. Like my son was always a year old. He never grew. She never grew either. They were on that shelf and I didn't tell them to grow. I told them to sit there. I'll be back. He was seventeen and she was fifteen. She wanted some answers. I was five years sober and I had taken my steps. I thought. I left them out. I didn't want anybody to know I was a bad father. I didn't want anybody to know I had kids. I lied in the beginning. I told everybody I don't have any family. They would ask me, "Well, where's your family at ?" I'd tell them I don't have one. That night it all changed.

I was in the process of getting the ABC Club licensed and certified. I had to go to some workshops in San Francisco. They were in south San Francisco, San Bruno. I went up to the workshops in the evening. I gave them my opinion. In order to work like this I believe you should be alcoholic. You got to be a drug addict, or an alcoholic, or they'll chew you up.

I went over to where my kids were. I knew where they were at. I always knew where they were at. They were at their stepfather's house. Their stepfather was my best friend. We went to school together. We knew everything about each other. He went into the service and I didn't get there. I tried, I tried everything, Marines, the Army, the Navy, the Coast Guard. I tried everything and each time it would come back 4F. I blamed God and the fact that I was stuttering. The truth was that I had weak lungs. I was hospitalized when I was seven years old for eighteen months. I had contacted tuberculosis from my father who died of it, besides alcoholism. The doctor told him if he laid on his back for six months in a hospital it would cure him. His buddies would come in every night and have a party there with him in the hospital. They killed him.

When I got older I went after his buddies. One of them had tuberculosis all through his legs. I wanted to kill him until I seen him, on crutches and all messed up. I told him to go F himself and turned around and left.

I don't know how I got to Alcoholics Anonymous, but I'm sure glad that I did. I was in Vacaville. I think everybody should go to Vacaville. They got a funny farm up there. There's a lot of funny people up there. Weird, weird. That's the second time I was in a psycho ward. I was in a psycho ward handcuffed to a bed. I've got a cop sitting on the end of the bed watching me, and everybody else in the ward was walking around, smoking cigarettes, and looking at me. I'm laying in that bed thinking, 'boy, there's a bunch of sickies in here.'

It ain't like that now. I hear they still have the psycho wards. I hear they still have the institutions. They're building new ones all the time. I've got my name on one of those bunks. They're waiting for me. I'm well aware of that, but not today. They might get me tomorrow, but not today.

I went to my first meeting in 1965. I was in isolation and the only way to get out of isolation is they called once a week for an AA meeting. So I got out of the cell to go to an AA meeting. I didn't go because I was interested in AA. I went because I was told there were free tailor made cigarettes and coffee. All the coffee you could drink and all the cigarettes you could smoke. I went because I needed something in my jacket. The inmates run the institutions, just in case you want to know.

Some people think the guards run the institutions, The guards don't run the institutions. The inmates run the institutions.

They were telling me, "You've got to get something in your jacket that looks good." I went to AA for three years. The day of the meeting I wouldn't drink no pruno (homemade hooch) or Aqua Velva aftershave, or put in any other mind altering chemicals in my body that I could get in there.

So I went. I sat in the back of the room, and I would listen and I wouldn't talk. I hated that word, alcoholic. I thought, 'Jesus that's my stepfather. He was the alcoholic, and my father was an alcoholic. But not me. I ain't that bad. I wouldn't identify myself. If anybody looked at me I'd give them the finger, or act like I was going to throw the coffee on them. The people that were leading the meeting got the idea, just leave that crazy guy alone back there. I took everybody's inventory. Just like you do back there. It's alright I understand.

I knew the first time I heard that word, alcoholic, that I was an alcoholic. I would not accept it. It took three more years going in-and-out of the meetings. I wouldn't drink, or take anything else the day of the meeting. I stopped the night before. I'd go to the meeting looking halfway presentable. Cigarettes, coffee, and me sitting in the back of the room and listening. I was listening and I was hearing stories I couldn't believe. People were talking about things I was taught you don't talk about. If they are true, or not. Don't put your garbage out on the street for anybody. Keep it buried. That's how I was raised.

I seen people coming into those institutions. They call it H & I (Hospitals and Institutions). There is an H & I Committee in the desert that meets. After you've been around long enough and you can get in a panel, I advise you to go. It's called action. Actions the magic word. Just going to meetings and sitting in the back of the room is not going to keep you sober. You've got to get involved and stay involved. It's called service. Service is very important.

After going in front of the penitentiary board three, or four times and getting turned down. I went in front of the board February 6th 1968. They asked me the year before, "We hear you're going to AA. If you found out your children were killed by a drunk driver, would you drink?" It stopped me cold. I couldn't answer that. They waited a couple of minutes, and then said, "Well, we are going to give you a year to think about that." I walked out of that door just cussing everybody out. Then the next year I was waiting for them. I went in the board room, and they didn't even ask me. They gave me a year date because I wasn't cooperating very well the first three years I was in there. I was sitting in the yard playing pinochle and dominos for cigarettes. If you never done that, you don't have to. I've seen people get killed for five packs of cigarettes. I've seen people get killed for chasing other peoples kids; some people call them punks. Some people call them queers. Whatever you want to call them.

An old guy in there told me two things you don't want to do. You don't want to gamble and you don't want to play around with homosexuals in the penitentiary. I did get one, but I didn't play around with the homosexuals. I come from a long line of gamblers. My grandfather was a bookie in San Francisco. He had a book in every cigar store in San Francisco. When he passed on my uncle and father took it over. My father was the baby of the family. My uncle used to use him like a wet rag, or something. So I've always had gambling in my blood. I still do. I just don't gamble one day at a time. For sure in this valley. It's enough being old. I don't want to be poor and old. There's nothing wrong with being poor. I've been poor. But I'd rather not be poor if I don't have to be. I'm not the kind of gambler that goes out and plays the penny poker machines all night long, and loses a quarter. Or wins a quarter.

One night I was up in Lake Tahoe. I brought my car that was paid off, the pink slip, and two pay checks. Three-thirty in the morning I'm out on the freeway. It's snowing and raining, and colder that hell, and I'm trying to hitchhike back to San Francisco. I'm cussing God out. You SOB look what you did to me. That's what kind of a gambler I am. I'm not a good gambler. It took me a lot of years to understand that, but I understand it today. I know God don't want me to be rich. He'll let me be comfortable but he won't let me be rich. He's probably got a hell of a good point there. Still I play the Lotto. I played the Lotto last week. The multi-million dollar one, and won 11 bucks. I thought it was wonderful. I bought one ticket. Costs $1 and won $11. So the next week I bought one more and didn't get one number.

Those people in those institutions got me. When I come out of Chino, It was raining. I think God is trying to tell me something. First I got out of the gate. I didn't want to get out of the gate. I was afraid to get out of the gate, because T Bow told me, "Man, why are you leaving? You're going to be back in two weeks."

I'd say, "F you, I am not." But down in my gut I knew I was going to go back. That was my pattern.

They called me and told me to roll it up. "You're going out." I ignored them. Usually when I do that they come and grab me and whip me over the head a few times, and put me into a hole for isolation. This time they came and got me and told me, "You're going." So I left. I think God intervened. God got me through that gate.

I got outside and one of the freemen, a guard there, says, "Danny get into my truck. I'll take you downtown and buy you your first drink."

I told him, "No thank you." I want to tell you it was because I had a spiritual program going. The fact is I didn't want to be seen in the truck with this guard. I didn't want anybody to think anything. I postponed it. I didn't want to start drinking in Chino. So, I thought, well maybe I'll wait until I get to Pomona. So I caught the bus to Pomona. The bus was late. I don't know how long it is to ride a bus from Pomona to Indio. We didn't get to Indio until five o'clock that night. It was late. It was raining. I was told in the institution to call AA and somebody would come and get me. I was scared. In those days the bus depot had a bar. There was a juke box going and the girls were in there. I made the call.

AA was in Indio. It was the old house. A person would say, "Hello?" I would start to say who I was. I was stuttering and the phone would go dead. I thought, sure you care. You think it's funny now, but at the time it wasn't a bit funny. I was really pissed off. I walked around there a little bit. This went on until 9 o'clock that night. I stayed out of that bar. That was another God shot. God was doing for me what I could not do for myself. I believe that. At 9 o'clock I was making two calls. I was calling the parole officer, who wasn't home, and AA who kept hanging up on me. I mean they hung up four, or five times. That pisses me off when somebody does that, so I called them back. I'm getting ready to put my money in the phone, and I looked up. It says dial your number and when someone answers the phone put your money in. I'd been locked up and I didn't know they changed that. So I called.

There was some old guy and three, or four other guys in the house. The manager went to bed at 7 o'clock. He'd go in his room and lock the door, and you wouldn't see him until seven the next morning. The guy that picked up the phone said that I was welcome to come over in the morning, and they were all going to bed. I thanked him. That seemed to be all that I needed. That got me over the hump. He told me how to get over here. I hung up. I made the other call. I got my parole officer on the phone. He told me to go downtown and get a room and come by my office in the morning. It was February 6th. The Fair was going on, and the Bob Hope Classic.

Indio was jumping downtown. People running up and down the street. The ladies were out doing whatever the ladies do out there. They invited me in the bars. I got through all that. I ended up in a room at the Potter Hotel. I thought it was the Fairmont Hotel. It was a big, big room. I thought it was wonderful. I went to bed, got up in the morning, came over to the club. Met the guys, and the guy who was running the club then. Had some coffee. I went down and met the agent that was in charge of me. He had a job waiting for me and I met the guy that I went to work for.

I hope you find what you are looking for. I hope you're not here just to get your court card signed. When I came in here they didn't have court cards. The parole officer told me if you behave yourself in six months we'll let you go back to San Francisco. After the six months he said, "You know you've been doing well. You ought to be able to go out on a Friday night and have a few." He didn't know anything about alcoholism. I let it go in one ear and out the other. I didn't listen to him. I listened to my sponsor, who I knew was trying to save my life. Help me save my life. I've had a lot of good sponsors. I've had Howard Bibby. I've had Bill M. Then Bill M came to work for us. Now I've got Alex. I love these guys. They are very important in my life. If you ain't got a sponsor, you better get one. Because you got a manic that lives in your head. I know a lot of you intellectual giants will not accept that fact. You ain't that bad.

Look around. If your sitting in the ABC Club at nine-fifteen at night looking at me up here at the podium, you've got a problem. I'm going to two memorials tomorrow; one at eleven and one at three. Glen is going to have a memorial at three at Saint Andrews Church. Also Don M who was involved in the Alano Club in Palm Spring for a lot of years. He helped a lot of drunks. At one time I knew everybody that was going to the Alano Club in Palm Springs. I knew everybody in AA in the valley.

Things have changed, there are hundreds, maybe thousands in the program, going to meetings that I don't know. That's okay I don't have to. It's not important. The only thing that's important is that I'm here. Doing what I do. I appreciate you all being here. I would not have wanted to be here. One of the guys I sponsor called me up and lied to me. He said the place was packed, and if you don't get down here you'll have to park your car two blocks away. I go speeding down the street thinking that will be the day, when I park two blocks away from the ABC Club. He's a good man. I sponsor a few people in here and they help me a lot more than I try to help them.

If you stay sober and you are going to get involved. That's what you are going to have to do. You can't just take, and take, and take, and take, and think you are going to stay sober. Your going to give it back. I believe that.

I made my amends to my son and he took a look at me and said, "Thank you, and no thank you." He was in school and he was fifteen-years old. He had his sports and he had his friends and he had his stepfather. He was not interested in me. I'd made my amends to his stepfather a few years before that. He wanted to meet at a bar in San Bruno. It's the San Bruno bowling alley. We sat in that bowling alley for three hours. He got drunk and I made my amends. When I walked in there I asked God to help me, and it worked. After it was over and we were leaving the bar. He said, "Danny I want you to come home and see the family."

I couldn't handle it. I thanked him and told him "No, I can't handle it." I had been up there three or four times before that. I got right up to the door, six o'clock in the morning,

We used to go on vacation, and we'd go up to Oregon. Helen's sister lives in Scottsdale, It's right outside Oregon. It's right outside Portland. We'd stop a mile away from where my children were. I'd get up at six in the morning and sneak out of the motel and run over there, and I'm going to knock on the door and present myself. I'd get right up to the door and I didn't have the guts enough to knock. I was too afraid. I was scared to death. So I'd have to turn around and go back and I'd feel all that guilt, and shame and other stuff. By the time I'd get back Helen would be up and asking, "Where were you?" I'd lie and say I was sitting in the coffee shop. I'd come back in with some donuts and some coffee. I told that lie for a long time. It was all taken care of.

My son and daughter's stepfather I tried to kill one night. I had him on the ground and I was really serious about killing him. My brother and a friend of his pulled me off of him. Thank God they did because I would have killed him that night. And then I was going to get her. It was all about looking good. I wasn't looking good and everybody knew it.

Everybody knew they were chasing around except me. I was too busy out chasing hamburgers. True story. I was told that later on. If you would have been home taking care of business like you were supposed to be, that never would of happened. We had, had a big church wedding We had five hundred people at the wedding. My father-in-law was a big shot. Boy, he put on a grand slam. I got drunk at the reception. Got into a fight. There was a big fight going on and we tore up the church. It wasn't a pretty sight. I shamed her, and I shamed her family. All I was doing was having a little fun I thought. I stopped doing all that. I try to act like a sober member of Alcoholics Anonymous.

I expect you people that are living in here to do the same. When you get here it's time to grow up. If you don't grow, you go. Everybody says he gets his rocks off, throwing you out. Telling you to pack your shit. Well, I don't. I don't like doing that, but I will do it. I'm known for doing it. From coast to coast.

I found a way how a manic, an asshole like me can survive in this world. It's called Alcoholics Anonymous. It's called surrendering. It's called getting on your knees everyday, everyday, everyday. It's the best thing I do. Give up. I know there's homies out there thinking, F him, I ain't going to do it. I am not going to do it. Then don't. Do it your way as long as you can. Don't give up until you absolutely have to.

I hope you heard something that will help you get through this day. Maybe tomorrow too.

My daughter, we have a great relationship. She married a yoyo. She had two children and one of them we brought down here because she is a lot like her grandpa. She damn near killed me while she was here. Drove me nuts. Trying to save her, trying to cure her. Don't work. They say you can't help your family. My son came down. He spent seventy-five days here and I helped him, or God helped him. Really God helped him and the people in the house did, and the people I sponsor did. A lot of you spent time with him.

My granddaughter is sixteen. I thought she was, but I called her mom and she just turned fifteen. That's how smart I am. They asked me a week ago to go by Wal-Mart and pick up a necklace they ordered. They put it in my name. For two weeks I've been procrastinating, I keep forgetting. Last night, after Nick and I went to a movie, on the way back I stopped there and picked it up. I put it in overnight this evening. So she should get it Monday.

I asked my grandson, who is eighteen, if he wanted me to send him a check, and he said, "No grandpa." I couldn't believe it. It amazed me. I asked my granddaughter who just turned fifteen. I asked her, "Do you want grandpa to send you a check?"

She said, "Sure grandpa."

It's great to laugh. If you can laugh at your disease there is hope for you. If you can't laugh at your disease you're in deep, deep, deep trouble. So my advice to you is start laughing your ass off.

CHAPTER 12

The Program

This information was formulated by Helen.

When you first came to the ABC Recovery Center and were admitted you were given the following hand outs:

Welcome. We know you are probably anxious and concerned about the circumstances which brought you here; we hope that you will be able to relax and remember that, like many before you, you have begun your journey into recovery from the disease of alcoholism/drug addiction.

Perhaps it will help you to know that every resident in this facility has an alcohol/drug problem. You may have other problems which you are reluctant to discuss: guilt, remorse, family, employment, financial, physical and spiritual. Don't worry you are not alone.

The staff and residents at the ABC Center are here to help you. Our staff is composed of a group of dedicated people who understand your illness, who have had a personal struggle with alcoholism/drug addiction. We hope that you will come to realize that alcoholism/drug addiction affects every segment of society. It is no disgrace to be an alcoholic/addict, the only disgrace is not to do something about it.

During the first thirty days here you are expected to find a sponsor and take the first steps. At the end of this time, an education assessment test will be given to determine whether you are able to attend school, or go to work. During the next sixty days you need to decide whether, or not you want to further your education through house tutorials, or outside academic, or vocational training classes. The center is determined to be as flexible as possible. We'll keep in mind admission date and when formal school classes begin. Some extra consideration of course will be given pregnant women. Generally however, it is not acceptable to begin educational development, here at ABC, beyond ninety days residency.

The program will help you but we will need your cooperation. Your attitude will play a very important part in your recovery program. We hope that you will listen, that you will ask questions, and that your stay in this program will be a rich, rewarding, learning experience which will move you toward recovery.

PROGRAM PHILOSOPHY

The staff of the ABC Center believes alcoholism/drug addiction is a disease that can be successfully treated. We also consider that alcoholism is not a mental disorder, nor is it a matter of morals, intellect or willpower and that the stigma often associated with alcoholism/drug addiction is both unwarranted and out-of-date.

We further believe that a person with the disease of alcoholism/drug addiction can no longer drink, or use socially. A return to drinking, or using at any point in the recovery phase must be viewed as a relapse of the disease, not a sign of failure of the individual, or the recovery program.

Our aim is to provide you with a non-drinking/using home environment that will give you the opportunity to help yourself. You can be assured that the ABC Center will not discriminate regardless of race, color, national origin, religion, creed, sex, mental, or a non-restrictive physical handicap. The program is based on the principals of Alcoholics Anonymous and Narcotics Anonymous.

ABC RECOVERY CENTER HOUSE
RULES AND PROCEDURES

While the ABC Recovery Center is not part of Alcoholics Anonymous, or Narcotics Anonymous, all residents will be introduced to and strongly encouraged to practice these principles. We feel this will be at the core of your sobriety and promote better relationships.

1. All residents must complete the required forms for our files.

2. During the first 30 days new residents are required to remain on the premises. Neither visitors, nor phone calls are allowed. Mail is, of course permitted (mail in front office till 5 p.m. then in back office). Note: 30 days is flexible. The figure is minimal restriction and depends upon each individual.

3. Room and board rates are $_____ per week, or the fee can be placed on a sliding scale. Residents, as soon as able, shall assume responsibility for room and board.

4. 1. Absolutely no alcohol or drugs; all life sustaining, medically prescribed drugs must be dispensed by staff. 2. No physical intimacy with residents of the opposite or same sex. 3. No violence, actual, or threatened, of any kind. THE INFRACTION OF ANY OF THESE RULES ARE CAUSE FOR IMMEDIATE DISMISSAL.

5. Residents are responsible for the cleanliness of their rooms as well as assisting with the keeping of common rooms and grounds.

6. Attendance at all AA/NA house meetings, groups and meals is required unless a resident is working, or in school. Attendance at outside meetings is encouraged once the resident is off restriction. Outside meetings may be substituted for house meetings.

7. Weekend passes and work will only be permitted when the resident has completed the restriction requirement and has done the first Three Steps of the AA/NA program with their sponsor. Weekend passes start after the Friday Night Speaker Meeting. Residents are required to return by Sunday at 7 p.m., or 5 p.m. on yard sale weekends (unless otherwise approved by staff).

8. All residents must sign out in the office before leaving the premises. Residents may leave with members of the opposite sex in odd number groups only. No pairing off.

9. No smoking permitted in any of the houses.

10. Profanity is considered to be an inadequate form of expression and is frowned upon.

11. Food or soft drinks are not permitted in the residents rooms, or the TV rooms in all houses. This includes candy, or snacks. (Residents under 30 days not permitted to operate TVs).

12. Residents under 30 days need special permission from the staff to attend outside meetings, however attendance at the Saturday night fellowship meeting is mandatory.

13. Valuables may be kept in the office safe. We are not responsible for money and valuables. Residents are not permitted to visit the rooms of other residents. Visitors must have staff permission and must be escorted by residents. No exceptions.

14. Residents, upon departure, must take all belongings with them. Space does not permit us to store personal belongings.

15. Staff must be notified when you have an outside appointment and it must be approved by staff. Sign out is a requirement. Schedule around groups and meetings. Write appointment time and date on calendar in back office.

16. Pornographic material is not allowed on the premises.

17. Walks with Danny are mandatory for residents under 30 days in the house.

Relapse Warning Signs

Relapse does not happen when the alcoholic takes the first drink. Relapse is a process that starts long before the alcoholic begins to drink. The relapse process causes the alcoholic to feel pain and discomfort when not drinking. The pain and discomfort can become so bad that the alcoholic becomes unable to live normally when not drinking. In AA this is called a dry drunk. Other people call it BUD (building up to drink). The discomfort can become so bad that the alcoholic feels that taking a drink can't be any worse than the pain of staying sober. The most commonly reported symptoms of relapse are described here:

Phase 1: Return of denial: During this phase the alcoholic/addict becomes unable to recognize, and honestly tell others what she/he is thinking, or feeling. The most common symptoms are:

1. Concern of well-being: The alcoholic feels uneasy, afraid, and anxious. At times she/he is afraid of not being able to stay clean. The uneasiness comes and goes and usually lasts only a short time.
2. Denial of the concern: In order to tolerate these periods of worry, fear, and anxiety, the alcoholic ignores, or denies these feelings in the way she/he had at one time denied alcoholism. The denial may be so strong that there is no awareness of the feeling, they are often forgotten as soon as the feelings are gone. It is only when the alcoholic thinks back about the situation at a later time that she/he is able to recognize the feelings of anxiety and the denial of those feelings.

Phase 2: Avoidance and defensive behavior: During this phase the alcoholic doesn't want to think about any thing that will cause the painful and uncomfortable feelings to come back. As a result, she/he begins to avoid anything, or anybody that will force an honest look at self. When asked direct questions about well-being, she/he tends to become defensive. The most common symptoms are:

3. Believing "I'll never drink again": The alcoholic convinces self that she/he will never drink again and sometimes will tell this to others, but usually keeps it to self. Many are afraid to tell their counselors, or other AA members about this belief. When the alcoholic firmly believes she/he will never drink again, the need for a daily recovery program seems less important.
4. Worrying about others instead of self: The alcoholic becomes more concerned about the sobriety of others than about personal recovery. She/he doesn't talk directly about these concerns, but privately judges the drinking of friends and spouse and the recovery programs of other recovering persons. In AA this is called 'working the other guy's program.'

5. Defensiveness: The alcoholic has a tendency to defend self when talking about personal problems, or his/her recovery program even when no defense is necessary.

6. Compulsive Behavior: The alcoholic becomes compulsive (stuck, or fixed, or rigid) in the way she/he thinks and behaves. There is a tendency to do the same things over and over again without a good reason. There is a tendency to control conversations either by talking too much, or not talking at all. She/he tends to work more than is needed, becomes involved in many activities and may appear to be the model of recovery because of heavy involvement in AA, Twelve Step work and chairing AA meetings. She/he is often a leader in counseling groups by playing therapist. Casual, or informal involvement with people, however, is avoided.

7. Impulsive Behavior: Sometimes the rigid behavior is interrupted by actions taken without thought, or self-control. This usually happens at times of high stress. Sometimes these impulsive actions cause the alcoholic to make decisions that seriously damage his/her life and recovery program.

8. Tendencies Toward Loneliness: The alcoholic begins to spend more time alone. She/he usually has good reasons, and excuses for staying away from other people. These periods of being alone begin to occur more often and the alcoholic begins to feel more and more lonely. Instead of dealing with the loneliness by trying to meet, and be around other people, behavior is more compulsive and impulsive.

Phase 3: During this phase the alcoholic begins experiencing a sequence of life problems that are caused by denying personal feelings, isolating self, and neglecting the recovery program. Even though she/he wants to solve these problems and works hard at it. Two new problems pop up to replace every problem that is solved. The most common symptoms are:

9. Tunnel Vision: Tunnel vision is seeing only one small part of life and not being able to get the 'big picture.' The alcoholic looks at life as being made up of separate, unrelated parts. She/he

focuses on one part without looking at the other parts or how they are related. Sometimes this creates the mistaken belief that everything is secure and going well. At other times this results in seeing only what is going wrong. Small problems are blown up and out of proportion. When this happens the alcoholic comes to believe she/he is being treated unfairly and has no power to do anything about it.

10. Minor Depression: Symptoms of depression begin to appear and to persist. The person feels down, blue, listless, empty of feelings. Oversleeping becomes common. She/he is able to distract self from these moods by getting busy with others things and not talking about the depression.

11. Loss of Constructive Planning: The alcoholic stops planning each day and the future. She/he often mistakes the AA slogan 'One day at a time,' to mean that one shouldn't plan, or think about what she/he is going to do. Less and less attention is paid to details. She/he becomes listless. Plans are based more on wishful thinking (how the alcoholic wishes things would be) than reality (how things really are).

12. Plans Begin to Fail: Because she/he makes plans that are not realistic and does not pay attention to details, plans begin to fail. Each failure causes new life problems. Some of these problems are similar to the problems that had occurred during drinking. She/he often feels guilty and remorseful when the problems occur.

Phase 4. Immobilization: During this phase the alcoholic is totally unable to initiate action. She/he goes through the motions of living, but is controlled by life rather than controlling life. The most common symptoms are:

13. Daydreaming and Wishful Thinking: It becomes more difficult to concentrate. The 'If only' syndrome becomes more common in conversation. The alcoholic begins to have fantasies of escaping, or 'being rescued from it all' by an event unlikely to happen.

14. Feeling That Nothing Can Be Solved: A sense of failure begins to develop. The failure may be real, or it may be imagined. Small failures are exaggerated and blown out of proportion. The belief that 'I've tried my best and sobriety isn't working out' begins to develop..

15. Immature Wish To Be Happy: A vague desire 'to be happy' or to have 'things work out' develops without the person identifying what is necessary to be happy or have things work out, 'magical thinking' is used: wanting things to get better without doing anything to make them better.

Phase 5. Confusion and Overreaction: During this period the alcoholic can't think clearly. She/he becomes upset with self and others, becomes irritable and overreacts to small things.

16. Periods of Confusion: Periods of confusion become more frequent, last longer, and cause more problems. The alcoholic often feels angry with self because of the inability to figure things out.

17. Irritation With Friends: Relationships become strained with friends, family, counselors, and AA members. The alcoholic feels threatened when these people talk about the changes in behavior and mood that are becoming apparent. The conflicts continue to increase in spite of the alcoholic's efforts to resolve them. The alcoholic begins to feel guilty and remorseful about his/her role in these conflicts.

Guilt

Guilt means that you use up your present moments being immobilized as a result of past behavior, while worry is the contrivance that keeps you immobilized in the **now**, about something in the future.

Your guilt is an attempt to change history, to wish that it weren't so, but history is so and you can't do anything about it.

You can begin to change your attitude about the things over which you experience guilt.

You can learn to savor pleasure without a sense of guilt. You can learn to see yourself as someone who is capable of doing anything that fits into your own value system and does not harm others--and doing it without guilt.

If you do something, whatever it may be, and you don't like it, or yourself after having done it, you can vow to eliminate such behavior for yourself in the future. But to go through a self inflicted guilt sentence is a neurotic trip you can bypass. The guilt does not help. It only keeps you immobilized, but it actually intensified the chances that you'll repeat the unwanted behavior. As long as you retain the potential payoff of absolving yourself with guilt, you'll be able to keep yourself in that vicious treadmill that leads to nothing but present moment unhappiness.

Guilt is the most useless of all feelings, it is by far the greatest waste of emotional energy. Why? Because, by definition, you are feeling immobilized in the present over something that has already taken place, and no amount of guilt can ever change history.

Guilt is not merely a concern with the past; it is a present moment immobilization about a past event. And the degree of immobilization can run from mild upset to severe depression. If repetition of some specific behavior, this is not guilt. You experience guilt only when you are prevented from taking action now as a result of having behaved in a certain way previously. Learning from your mistakes is healthy and a necessary part of growth. Guilt is unhealthy because you are ineffectively using up your energy in the present feeling hurt, upset and depressed about a historical happening. And it's futile as well as unhealthy. No amount of guilt can ever undo anything.

Here are the most basic reasons for choosing to waste your present feeling guilty about things that you've done, or failed to do in the past.

1. Guilt is an avoidance technique for working on yourself in the present. Thus you shift responsibility for what you are, or are not now, to what you were, or were not in the past.

2. By shifting responsibility backward, it is easier to immobilize yourself with guilt about the past than to take the hazardous path of growing in the present.

3. There is a tendency to believe that if you feel guilty enough, you will eventually be exonerated for having been naughty.

4. Guilt can be a means of returning to the safety of childhood, a secure period when others made decisions for you and took care of you. The payoff is in being protected from having to take charge of your own life.

5. Guilt is a useful method for transferring responsibility for your behavior from yourself to others.

6. Often you can will the approval of others even when those others don't approve of your behavior by feeling guilt for that behavior.

7. Guilt is a superb way to win pity from others. No matter that the desire for the pity is a clear indication of low self-esteem. In this case you'd rather have others feel sorry for you, than like and respect yourself.

There you have the most notorious of the dividends for hanging onto guilt. Guilt, like all self-nullifying emotions, is a choice, something that you exercise control over.

Some strategies for eliminating guilt:

1. Begin to view the past as something that can never be changed, despite how you feel about it. It's over! "My feeling guilty will not change the past, nor will it make me a better person." This sort of thinking will help you to differentiate guilt from learning as a result of your past.

2. Ask yourself what you are avoiding in the present with guilt about the past. By going to work on that particular thing, you will eliminate the need for guilt.

3. Begin to accept certain things about yourself that you've chosen, but which others may dislike. It is necessary that you approve of

yourself, the approval of others is pleasant, but beside the point. Once you no longer need approval, the guilt for behavior which does bring approval will disappear.

4. Keep a Guilt Journal, and write down any guilty moments, noting precisely when, why, and with whom it occurs, and what you are avoiding in the present with this agonizing over the past.

5. Reconsider your value system. Which values do you believe in and what do you only pretend to accept? List all of these phony values and resolve to live up to a code of ethics that is self-determined, not one that has been imposed by others.

6. Make a list of all the bad things you've ever done. Give yourself guilt points for each of them on a scale of one to ten. Add up your score and see if it makes any difference in the present whether it's one hundred, or one million. The present moment is still the same and all of your guilt is merely wasteful activity.

7. Assess the real consequences of your behavior. Rather than looking for a mystical feeling to determine yes's and no's in your life, determine whether the results of your actions are pleasing and productive for you.

8. Teach those in your life who attempt to manipulate you with guilt that you are perfectly capable of handling their disappointment in you. Once you de-fuse the guilt, the emotional control over you and the possibility of manipulating are eliminated forever.

9. Do something which you know is bound to result in feelings of guilt. These kinds of behavior will help you to tackle that omnipresent guilt that so many sectors of the environment are adept at helping you to choose.

Such is guilt in our culture--a convenient tool for manipulating others are a futile waste of time. Worry, the other side of the coin, is diagnostically identical to guilt, but focuses exclusively on the future and all of the terrible things that might happen.

Made in the USA
Las Vegas, NV
11 February 2021